A SURVIVAL KIT
FOR TAXPAYERS

A SURVIVAL KIT FOR TAXPAYERS

STAYING ON GOOD TERMS WITH THE I.R.S.

Revised Edition

ROBERT S. HOLZMAN, Ph.D.

COLLIER BOOKS

A Division of Macmillan Publishing Co., In...

New York

COLLIER MACMILLAN PUBL...

London

Macmillan Publishing Co., Inc.
866 Third Avenue, New York, N.Y. 10022
Collier Macmillan Canada, Ltd.

Library of Congress Cataloging in Publication Data
Holzman, Robert S.
A survival kit for taxpayers.
Includes index.
1. Tax administration and procedure—United
States.   2.   United States.   Internal Revenue Service.
I. Title.

| KF6300.H64 1981 | 343.73′04 | 81-11828 |
| ISBN 0-02-008270-3 | 347.3034 | AACR2 |

10 9 8 7 6 5 4 3 2 1

Printed in the United States of America

TO THE
COMMISSIONER OF INTERNAL REVENUE
*without whose persistent interest in
my affairs, this book never would
have been written*

Contents

Foreword to the Revised Edition

Not long ago, a distinguished historian wrote an in-depth biography of President William McKinley. This book, wrote one reviewer, contains more information about McKinley than anyone would possibly want to know.

That same observation could be made generally of books written by former Revenue Agents about the Internal Revenue Service. Readers are apt to find that these books contain more about the I.R.S. than any taxpayer would care or need to know. He is interested in the relevancy of the tax laws and their administration to *him*. Period. This is what the present book provides. It is concerned with what a taxpayer *must* do and what is highly desirable that he *should* do in such areas as learning his obligations, where he can get help and the extent to which he can rely upon it, what records he must keep and for how long, what a Revenue Agent can or cannot request or do, what the alternatives are when there is a tax disagreement. It highlights tax traps and pitfalls, such as saying too much or being the strong, silent type.

Here is practical help on how to be a good taxpayer, not merely because of patriotism or morality or fear, but because it makes sound business sense. By being a good taxpayer, fully knowledgeable as to your obligations and your rights, you may legitimately save time, money, and aggravation.

Legalistically, a personal income tax may appear to be a tax upon *income*. But in reality, it is a tax on *people*. And that is what this volume is about: people, specifically, taxpayers. This book is concerned, not with the I.R.S. and its tax collectors, but with taxpayers. *We are on your side.*

Preface

One of these days, it is likely that you will be having a confrontation session with an Internal Revenue Agent. Such an experience never has been regarded as pleasant. Typically, one British lady wrote in a book which was published in 1850, "There is something transcendently disgusting in an income tax which not only takes a substantial sum immediately out of a man's pocket but compels him to expose his affairs to a party [a Revenue official] that he would by no means choose for a confidant."

It is the purpose of the present book to ensure that your relations with the Internal Revenue Service will be less distressing than that. If you are aware of what is expected of you, how to prepare currently so that you will be ready when that confrontation session comes, what to do when you and the I.R.S. cannot agree, what pitfalls are to be avoided, and what the Service already knows about you (plenty!) the day of reckoning need not be a traumatic experience for you.

Remember how differently you felt, during carefree childhood, about going to school when you were confident that you had done your homework well. Just *let* the teacher call my name! After putting into use the practical recommendations contained in this book, you may now enjoy again the same satisfaction of knowing that you are well prepared for whatever happens when your name is called (make that "printed out") by the Internal Revenue Service computers.

Many Happy Returns!

A SURVIVAL KIT
FOR TAXPAYERS

Income Tax Appeal Procedure
Internal Revenue Service

At any stage of procedure:

Agreement and payment may be arranged.

Requests for issuance of a notice of deficiency to allow petition to the Tax Court may be made.

The tax may be paid and a refund claim filed.

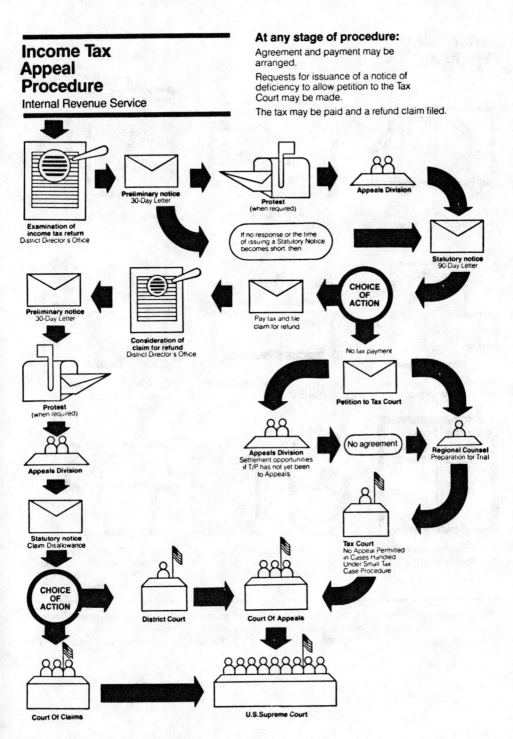

Prepared by the Internal Revenue Service

Processing Pipeline

Returns are delivered to the Regional Service Centers.

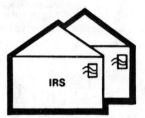

Envelopes are opened and counted.

Returns are sorted by type of return.

Tax returns and accompanying checks are compared.

Returns are edited and coded for computer processing.

Tax return information is placed on magnetic tape for computer processing.

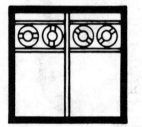

IRS computers check returns for mathematical accuracy.

Tapes are sent to the National Computer Center for Account Posting and Settlement.

Tapes of Refunds are sent to the Treasury Department Disbursing Center for issuance of checks directly to taxpayers.

Once a tax return reaches one of ten IRS Service Centers, it travels through a series of processing steps known as "the pipeline."

While many parts of the pipeline shown here are automated for faster processing and faster refunds, people are involved every step of the way.

1.
The Tax on Inability to Satisfy the Revenue Agent

It is called an income tax, but it can be far more than that deceptively simple label suggests. What a person really is taxed upon may be his ignorance, or his carelessness, or his inability to meet the obligations of being a taxpayer.

If you do not know what records you have to keep, or how "income" may be taxed because you cannot show that for various reasons what came in actually was not income, or that deductions can be disallowed merely because you did not know how long records had to be kept, your tax is not being based upon income. One's federal income tax liability depends to a major extent upon his awareness of what his tax obligations are.

The distinguished Mr. Justice Holmes declared in a Supreme Court decision that "taxes are what we pay for civilized society." How much civilization are you required to pay for? A person's first federal income tax responsibility is to find out. Unfortunately, the law does not say how. But, in the words of one court, "the taxpayer is presumed to know the law and the provisions of the law."

In a case which happened to involve a well-known dancing teacher, a judge announced that "the rendering of a proper return should be regarded by every citizen as a vital part of his life equally with that of attention to his business." The plain fact of the matter is that taxes *are* your business. A person who is only moderately successful, in a financial sense, probably spends more on taxes than on anything else. So the largest part of his business activities is devoted to earning his tax money. If he pays too much in taxes, he is shortchanging himself and his family. If he pays too little, predictably he will learn some of the many ways in which the Internal Revenue Service can show its displeasure.

This applies equally in the case of state and local taxes. In the words of one court, a person "is presumed to know the general public laws of her place of residence and the legal effects of her acts."

A person cannot avoid penalty where income has been understated on his tax return by blaming the accountant who prepared it. As the court noted in a 1980 decision, an individual "must shoulder the ultimate responsibility of providing sufficient, accurate information to allow the return preparer an opportunity to prepare a correct return. . . . [The taxpayers] did not meet their initial obligation of providing accurate information to [the accountant]."

A businessperson can't avoid penalty for failure to maintain proper tax records by telling his accountant to do whatever is necessary. In the words of one decision, "The mere placing of a tabulation of his books and records in the hands of his accountants and thereafter giving no more of his personal attention to the question of the filing of required returns does not appear to us to be the exercise of ordinary business care and prudence."

Knowing *how much* to pay in federal income taxes is the business of every person. In the language of one judicial decision, "The government is not charged with the duty . . . of functioning as a tax advisor. It is the taxpayer's responsibility to ascertain his obligations."

At the start of the Battle of Trafalgar, Admiral Nelson sent this message to his fleet: "England expects every man to do his duty." The modern income tax was born as the result of the Napoleonic wars of that period, and one of the duties expected (required) today is the paying of taxes. But it is no simple matter to find out what is required. The Internal Revenue Service issues instructions intended to convey this information, such as is most commonly needed for an individual's federal income tax form, known by its number of 1040. According to a report by the Comptroller General of the United States in 1978, "The experts determined that the 1040 instructions are written at a medium reading level of the 10th grade. This level is above the reading skills of perhaps 13 million, or one-fifth, of the taxpayers who must use them."

How to Meet the Obligations of Being a Taxpayer

A person can get help in fulfilling his federal income tax responsibilities in one of three ways. Each has very serious shortcomings.

1. *He can seek the assistance of the Internal Revenue Service.* The Service is very generous in its efforts to be helpful. Typically, the packet of federal income tax forms sent to taxpayers for filing in 1980 contained a letter over the signature of the Commissioner of Internal Revenue him-

self, which stated in part, "If you need help, please call us at the number listed for your area on page 46, or visit an IRS office."

What happens if you do call? You may be given an answer to your question by a pleasant person who clearly is trying strenuously to be helpful to you. Yet what he or she says will lack any acceptability whatsoever as far as the Internal Revenue Service is concerned, if he or she actually does not possess the authority to answer the question. In one case, the Service, when examining a taxpayer's return, refused to accept as correct an answer given to a taxpayer by an employee in the tax office who had the impressive title of Conferee-Reviewer in the Coordination and Advisory Section of the Practice and Procedures Division. Actually, he was supposed to be working on research duties for the Internal Revenue Service and not expressing opinions to taxpayers. But how could they be expected to know the limitations of his responsibility?

In 1973, the Report of the Legal and Monetary Affairs Subcommittee of the House of Representatives Committee on Government Operations noted that the Internal Revenue Service invites taxpayers to seek its aid. Continued the report, "This put the IRS in a contradictory posture. While encouraging the public to utilize its representatives, the IRS tells taxpayers who do so not to rely on the assistance received."

But what most frequently prevents a taxpayer from getting a correct answer from the Internal Revenue Service is sheer numbers. Millions of other persons also have received this kind invitation from the Commissioner and seek to take advantage of it. There simply is not enough time for earnest, hard-working I.R.S. personnel to get into the guts of your own personal tax problem and to furnish responses which are entirely correct in all instances. For example, one person asked if she could deduct the cost of an ear operation. Yes, she was told correctly, to the extent that the expense of this operation and all other genuine medical bills for that year exceeded 3% of her adjusted gross income. So she deducted the amount in accordance with this answer to her question. When her tax return was audited, the deduction was disallowed, and she was assessed additional tax, penalty, and interest. What she had failed to tell the Service employee was that an insurance company had reimbursed her for the cost of the operation, which consequently had not been her expense at all. And her well-intentioned I.R.S. advisor did not have time to ask questions or to explain the exceptions to that general rule as to medical expense deductions. *You have to know enough about the tax law to understand what questions to ask.* There is no one to tell you this.

As the court declared when this taxpayer protested the treatment she had received, "Each year the Internal Revenue Service provides information and assistance to millions of taxpayers on an informal basis. Its employees cannot be expected to be correct as to every question asked or held to a standard of infallibility, especially when all the facts may not have been fully presented."

During 1979, the Internal Revenue Service received about 96 thousand written, 33 million telephone, and 8 million walk-in inquiries.

Actually the result is no different even when information is given on a formal basis. An internationally prominent corporation wanted to exchange some of its own stock for shares in another company, H, in order to acquire this second company. Such an exchange, under appropriate circumstances, could have taken place so that the shareholders of H would not be taxed upon this exchange of stock. In order to persuade the H shareholders to agree to make the exchange, the well-known corporation sent a lengthy request for a ruling, with a statement of all of the facts, to the Internal Revenue Service. In time, the Service wrote back that the H shareholders could exchange their stock without federal income tax liability. In reliance upon this written ruling, the H shareholders agreed to make the exchange and did so. Five years later, the Internal Revenue Service changed its mind and revoked its ruling as to non-taxability. Each H shareholder was assessed tax upon his transaction. Many costly lawsuits were required to determine the tax status of persons who had relied upon this ruling.

In one case where an individual protested the unfairness of having a tax disallowance after he had followed the interpretation given by the tax office, a court observed that "we find it commendable for him to seek the assistance of the Internal Revenue Service in the preparation of [the form]. At a time when taxpayers are encouraged by the Commissioner to seek the assistance of the Internal Revenue Service in the preparation of their tax returns it may appear to [him], and we can appreciate his viewpoint, unfair that erroneous advice by the Internal Revenue Service is not binding on the Commissioner of Internal Revenue." But, "regretfully," the court upheld the assessment.

One decision concerned a taxpayer who wrote to the Internal Revenue Service to ask the last day a request could be made for a court review of a tax assessment. The I.R.S. erroneously wrote back a date that was one week later than the proper date. Neither the Service nor the court could do anything about allowing his request for a review which arrived after the permissible date, although it had been the Service that had goofed—in writing.

A party may ask the proper questions and present all of the facts correctly to an Internal Revenue Service employee. The tax return as filed is incorrect if an incorrect answer is given to his request. Who is responsible? The responsibility is that of the person whose signature appears on the tax return, that is, the taxpayer. It is *his* tax return, and any errors on it are *his*. The fact that an I.R.S. employee delegated to answer questions gave an improper response does not change the meaning of something provided in the tax law. Only Congress can write a federal law. If a government employee tells you something which is contrary to what the law says, he is in fact writing or rewriting a tax law. As the celebrated Judge Learned Hand wrote in a frequently quoted decision, ". . . harsh as it may be, one accepts the advice of a revenue official at his peril."

It was pointed out in a recent case that requests for rulings from the Internal Revenue Service generally are not issued until about ten weeks after submission of the requests, and delays may be more than three months if more than one branch of the Service is involved. But a controversial question, such as deductibility of home office expenses, may require several years for a ruling.

It does not matter how lofty a position is held by the tax official who answers your question. If the answer given is incorrect, it does not make any difference what the rank of the person giving it may be. That is what the court said in the case of a United States senator who was important enough to bring his question directly to the top tax official in the land, the Commissioner of Internal Revenue himself. His reply, in writing, was contrary to what the law said. The Commissioner could not change the law. Neither could the court. So the Commissioner's interpretation was overturned by one of his own very junior employees, with court approval. The record does not indicate the fate of that junior employee.

2. *He can pay for the assistance of a professional tax advisor.* In 1977, the Roper Organization, Inc., an opinion polling firm, interviewed a nationwide cross section of adults. About 54% of those persons who filed federal income tax returns said they went to professional preparers, the chief reason being because the requirements for paying taxes and the instructions for the form were too difficult to understand.

Printed on the packet of tax forms which the Internal Revenue Service sent to taxpayers one year were these words: "If you decide to have someone else prepare your return, select a qualified person." Ah, but how does a person do that? In one case where an individual argued that he had relied upon an expert advisor, the court concluded that employment by the Internal Revenue Service for a couple of years did not qualify the person who gave the advice "as a tax expert."

It is becoming increasingly important, if you use a professional tax preparer, to follow the government's advice and "select a qualified person." If audit by the I.R.S. discloses errors in your own favor, you are the one who pays the tax deficiency, penalty, and interest. But the danger goes far beyond this. Many tax preparers are incompetent and some are downright dishonest. They may create additional dependents for you to claim, or invent imaginary church contributions appearing on your return, and the like. That can result in very severe fraud penalties. The Internal Revenue Service knows, of course, that this sort of thing is going on. So the Service sends its own agents disguised as taxpayers (an easy part to play) to numerous tax preparers, in order to present pretended facts for use in the preparation of a federal income tax return. If a professional preparer shows gross incompetency, reckless disregard of the tax laws and regulations or dishonesty, there are various unpleasant things which will happen to him. But the taxpayer also may be in trouble. All tax returns which had been prepared by this particular professional person are now suspect. The I.R.S. has authority to get from him a list of all parties whose tax returns he had prepared. Now gimlet-eyed Revenue Agents, who have definite reason to suspect that your tax return is improper—or worse—will descend upon you. This will not be a casual, routine examination. You will not enjoy it.

Some tax preparers guarantee clients that if any penalty is assessed against a return, the preparer himself will absorb this charge. But that does not mean that the client is not hurt. A person is taxed upon the amount of any obligation which someone else pays for him. The penalty is yours because it is the result of entries on *your* tax return. So the preparer's assumption of the penalty represents taxable income to his client.

3. *He can seek services that are offered to him without charge.* Some individuals contribute generously of their expertise to help people who cannot afford to pay for aid. For example, a businessperson may participate in the Volunteer Income Tax Assistance (VITA) program. This is an ongoing program established under the auspices of the Internal Revenue Service to help taxpayers comply with the tax laws and meet their obligations. Free assistance is provided to low-income, elderly, and non–English-speaking persons in the preparation of their returns. The I.R.S. trains the VITA volunteers. But regardless of how successful a volunteer may have been in his own business, it does not follow that he is equally knowledgeable in the area of income taxes. The value of the services of

willing, sympathetic volunteers obviously varies from person to person.

4. *He can handle his own taxes on a do-it-yourself basis.*

The federal income tax law takes the form of a mammoth, complex compilation of rules which are changing constantly and which are being re-interpreted by the courts without letup. If a person seriously tries to become a master of taxation, he will have little time to do anything else, such as run his business or manage his household. And though his intelligence level may be very high, his background and temperament may not equip him for this sort of thing.

He may seek to understand those parts of the tax law and the so-called Treasury Department regulations which are appplicable to him by reading the concise, simplified explanations which are prepared by Internal Revenue Service experts for the person in the street. Unfortunately, these simplified explanations frequently are so oversimplified for easy comprehension that important exceptions or unusual circumstances are not mentioned at all. There is one sentence in the Internal Revenue Code which is thirty-seven lines long in print. Any restatement of this in layman's language predictably will leave out something which is contained in the actual law. In one case, an individual made a plea in court, "If I cannot rely on the . . . IRS instructions, what can I rely on?" The judge admitted that this plea "has strong appeal." But the taxpayer lost anyway, because it is the law and not the Service instruction which is the authoritative statement of what is required.

Sometimes the Internal Revenue Service publications, which were designed to help taxpayers, make the language of the tax law even more confusing. It was stated by a judge in a 1978 decision that "Whoever drafted that language evidently thought that by restating the statutory test in negative terms, he was improving the understandability of the statute." That the I.R.S.'s contribution to understanding what the law actually said only confused the taxpayer about what, in the court's words, the law "clearly" declares did not save him a disallowance.

The Comptroller General of the United States declared in a 1978 report, "Certainly, the accuracy of the forms and instructions has no value unless people understand what is said."

In one case, an individual sought to show that what the Internal Revenue Service had disallowed on his tax return was completely in accord with instructions published by this same Service. But it was held that he was bound by what was said in the law and not by imprecise language of oversimplified instructions, which are intended to be merely explanatory and not complete. In order to see what the law really provides, added this court unhelpfully, one should consult the voluminous Internal Revenue Code, the ever-changing Treasury Department regulations, and administrative rulings which are published—and amended—regularly in the *Federal Register*. Of course, it was just to avoid full-time research by taxpayers that the Internal Revenue Service explanatory publications were issued. The government's own excellent booklet for taxpayer guidance, *Your Federal Income Tax,* which is thoroughly updated each year, similarly is not accepted by the courts or even by its own authors, the I.R.S., as an authority for what is printed there. Ruled one court, "Such informal publication is not a source of authoritative law in the tax field."

A common illustration of this is a contribution to a charitable, religious, educational, or similar organization. The Internal Revenue Service publishes periodical listings of organizations, contributions to which are deductible for tax purposes up to specified limits. When a person is considering the making of a contribution to a particular organization, or the preparation of his federal income tax return, he should consult this list to ascertain whether the organization is in good standing for this purpose. But by the time his tax return is audited, the charitable organization's name may have been removed from the approved listing. In order to be entitled to a contributions deduction, the Service expects that a donor large enough to be heeded by the organization will obtain from it an affirmative statement that this organization is not engaging in any form of discrimination which could result in loss of tax-exempt status.

Contributions to an Individual Retirement Account (IRA) are deductible within certain limits. But no deduction is allowed if for any part of the year a person was covered by an employer-financed pension plan. One individual was penalized for claiming a deduction for a payment into an IRA earlier in the year, before he was hired by a corporation that had a pension plan. He claimed that nothing was said in I.R.S. Publication 590, *Tax Information on Individual Retirement Savings Programs* about loss of deduction by a person who later in the year went to work with a company having a pension plan. So, he argued, he should not be penalized by reason of the fact that the Service had misled him by not telling him the whole story. You shouldn't have relied on a simplified I.R.S. explanation, chided the court in a 1980 decision. If you had turned to the voluminous law itself, you could have seen how the Service had oversimplified the explanation.

A person who wants to keep current on the constant changes which are being made in the federal tax field as a result of recent rulings and interpretations may subscribe to the Treasury Department's *Internal Revenue*

Bulletin, at a far lower cost than the loose-leaf services which are published by several commercial firms, for these services also include a considerable amount of other material. This *Bulletin* publishes new rulings, administrative procedures and practices, and statements of the latest policy. A feature is the presentation of brief summaries of each ruling or decision, in layman's language, as prepared by the Internal Revenue Service itself. But there is printed in each issue of the *Bulletin* this disclaimer: "These summaries are intended only as aids to the reader in identifying the subject matter covered. They may not be relied upon as authoritative interpretations."

For that you must seek out the official text of the law itself. But make certain that you see the latest version. And even if you have before you the actual language of the law as written by Congress, the meaning is apt to be anything but clear. According to a senior editor of *Reader's Digest,* which enjoys an enviable reputation for presenting complex materials in a manner which its own readers easily can understand, the federal income tax law "has to be one of the most daunting documents a citizen is obliged to read."

The taxpayer who wishes to handle his returns on a do-it-yourself basis may wonder why it is not reasonable to expect Congress to write our laws so that they can be understood by the persons who are affected by them. In some important areas, but not the tax law, people now are being required to communicate legal language intelligibly. The Pension Reform Act of 1974 provides that a description of each employer's plan "shall be furnished to participants. . . . The summary plan description . . . shall be written in a manner calculated to be understood by the average plan participant. . . ." The New York State General Obligations Law directs that apartment leases signed after November 1, 1978, must be "written in a clear and coherent manner using words with common and everyday meanings." But the person who wishes to prepare his own federal income tax return must realize that Congress has not yet accepted the responsibility of writing tax laws "in a manner calculated to be understood by the average [taxpayer]." Or even by the far-above-average taxpayer.

Some relief for the do-it-yourself taxpayer may be on the way, but it appears to be some years before anything will be done about it. A little-noted provision in the Revenue Act of 1978 states that the Secretary of the Treasury is required to submit a report to Congress by November 6, 1980, of (1) the provisions of the Internal Revenue Code "which, due to their complexity, may hamper the ability of individuals to prepare and complete federal income tax returns, and (2) methods of simplifying federal income tax return forms and instructions." On the basis of this report, it is up to Congress to decide what, if anything, is to be done about it. In view of the size and intricacies of the existing tax law, the translation of this report into understandable language will take much time and effort. Meanwhile, there will be more tax returns which have to be filed under existing law.

Upon Whom Can One Rely?

You probably can get by without knowing how the transmission on your car works. You may never need to know how your own digestive process functions. But an individual must understand enough about his own tax situation to recognize when he is in need of assistance, be knowledgeable enough to choose an advisor, and know what to tell the advisor.

Nothing that anyone tells you will relieve you of your proper tax liability. If tax has been understated, you still owe the correct amount, regardless of who advised you to the contrary. But penalty for a tax deficiency may be waived if a person can show that (1) he had made a full disclosure of all of the relevant facts (2) to a party competent to advise him and (3) he had relied upon the advice which he was furnished when he prepared the tax return. All of these elements have to be proven in order to avoid penalty. That puts a premium upon knowing what requires advice and who is equipped to provide it.

About the best that can be said about advice from the Internal Revenue Service which takes the form of a ruling is that it may be better to have a ruling than not to have one. Even if a taxpayer can get a ruling from the Service, there is no assurance that it will not be revoked, perhaps retroactively. In one decision, a taxpayer received a ruling from the I.R.S. that a certain deduction was proper, and returns were filed in reliance upon this written answer to a specific question. But the deduction was disallowed, because the Service subsequently published a general ruling which took a contrary point of view. The court emphasized that it was not unreasonable to impose upon a taxpayer receiving a favorable ruling the responsibility of keeping abreast of current developments to be assured that the ruling continued to be in effect.

Even when the Internal Revenue Service writes to you that you can do something, you may not be allowed to. In one case, the Service wrote to a taxpayer that he could request a refund within a specified time, which happened to be incorrect. While deploring the Service's erroneous letter, a court refused to agree to this extra time for filing the claim.

Under a union-employer contract, all employers had to make certain contributions to the union pension fund of stated percentages of each employee's salary. One employee sought to deduct contributions made by his employer to this fund as an expense in connection with his employment. When the deduction was challenged by the I.R.S., he pointed to the 1976 edition of the Service's own publication, *Your Federal Income Tax,* which stated that "old age pension fund assessments paid to remain in the union and to hold a job are deductible." That means amounts paid by union members, not by their employers such as here, countered the Service. That's not what your own explanation book says, persisted the taxpayer. He lost. In a 1980 decision, the court held that even if the "explanatory" government book printed those words, they were a mere interpretation of the law. What the law really says, not what the I.R.S. book declares, is what counts.

A favorable ruling addressed to another taxpayer cannot be utilized by anyone else, even if the facts appear to be identical.

You cannot rely upon an interpretation of what a law means even when the congressman who had written that very law has explained what he had in mind. As the United States Supreme Court has stated, "The remarks of a single legislator, even the sponsor [of a bill], are not controlling in analyzing legislative history."

There are many questions, referred to as "prime issues," on which the Internal Revenue Service declines to render a ruling. In addition, the Service generally will not issue a ruling unless the taxpayer submits all facts and the transaction already has taken place. Inasmuch as a copy of this ruling is sent to the I.R.S. district office where the taxpayer files his income tax return, this means that if the ruling should prove to be unfavorable, the matter automatically will be referred to the Revenue Agent who has now been alerted to disallow it.

The Burden of Proof

It was mentioned at the start of this chapter that the so-called income tax frequently amounts to a tax on the inability to satisfy the Internal Revenue Service. Inasmuch as the burden of proof in a tax matter almost always is upon the taxpayer (see Chapter 3), failure for any reason to prove an item on the tax return will result in additional tax. Various presumptions against the taxpayer, moreover, can result in taxes. It has been held by the courts that an unexplained loss of records, such as checkbooks or contributions receipts, carries a strong presumption that the misplacement or destruction had been deliberate, for the taxpayer's benefit. Failure of a taxpayer to keep proper books and records of his income-producing activities gives the Internal Revenue Service the right to use the best evidence available in order to determine taxable income, such as concluding that any apparent increase in net worth was due to unreported taxable income. When a person dies, his safe-deposit box in a bank cannot be opened until a tax official is present to take inventory; and any cash in this box is presumed to represent previously unreported income unless there is creditable evidence to the contrary. A taxpayer's death is, in fact, likely to result in additional income taxes, for he no longer is present to explain perfectly legitimate transactions or to unearth supporting evidence which is required to substantiate a tax deduction.

2.
Why Me?

Nobody likes a tax audit, except a Revenue Agent. Even if your return is a very simple one, the figures are very modest, and you have carefully maintained records of everything relevant, an audit is likely to mean anxiety. Perhaps, inadvertently, you *have* been doing something incorrectly. Or a necessary piece of supporting evidence may have gotten lost. Or the Internal Revenue Service may be looking for an income item which erroneously was reported by somebody to have been paid to you. The process can be time-consuming, even if everything is in order. If other people learn that your tax return is being audited, that might suggest that you are some sort of criminal type.

"The vast majority of taxpayers are honest and have nothing to fear from an examination of their tax returns," states an Internal Revenue Service announcement. "An examination of such a taxpayer's return does not even suggest a suspicion of dishonesty or criminal liability. It may not even result in more tax. Many cases are closed without change in reported tax liability and, in many others, the taxpayer receives a refund."

All that may sound very reassuring. But no one wants to be audited anyway. When the Internal Revenue Service shows a deep interest in one's affairs, he will want to know why he was singled out for this treatment.

How Tax Returns Are Selected for Audit

Federal income tax returns are checked routinely for mechanical accuracy by Internal Revenue Service computers. It is stated in the 1979 *Annual Report of the Commissioner of Internal Revenue* that "the Computer Center operates twenty-four hours a day, seven days a week . . ." Taxpayers are notified of additional amounts owed by them, or refunds, as a result of these changes. Appeals cannot be made to the United States Tax

17

Court or to any other body at this point, because there is nothing to argue about.

The usual reason for selecting a tax return for examination is to verify the correctness of income, deductions, or exemptions that have been reported by the taxpayer. Returns are selected for examination primarily by the use of a computer program known as Discriminant Function System, or DIF. This is a mathematically based system which involves the assignment of weights to the entries on tax returns and the production by computer of a score for each return. The Internal Revenue Service is not anxious to waste manpower (peoplepower) on an audit where the statistical probability of recovering enough in tax deficiencies to pay for the cost of the audit is unpromising. So as a result of extensive and highly confidential studies made by the I.R.S., it is determined how much a person in each income range is likely to spend on interest, medical expenses, contributions, state and local taxes, and the like. If he claims deductions for more than is to be expected in the light of his income, there is a probability that there are tax errors on the return. The higher the score in the light of possible errors such as might be indicated by excessive medical expenses, etc., the greater the possibility of error in a return. Returns identified by DIF as "ostensibly improper deviations from the tax laws" (to use I.R.S. technical jargon) are then screened manually, and those confirmed as having the highest error potential are selected for examination.

Returns also may be selected for audit as part of the random samples under the Taxpayer Compliance Measurement Program (TCMP), which is the Service's long-range program designed to measure and to evaluate taxpayer compliance characteristics. Information obtained by the I.R.S. from TCMP is used to update and to improve DIF.

If you use a tax shelter, have vague or missing records, claim unusually large business entertainment deductions, or are uncooperative with a Revenue Agent, you can expect to receive a mighty thorough examination of every single item on your tax return, because the Internal Revenue Service has reason to suspect the worst of you. But if the Service computers randomly spew forth your number, an honest, cooperative person who clearly keeps the most careful records will be subjected to the same intensive, time-consuming, you-gotta-prove-every-cent procedure as an obvious tax dodger. Under TCMP, tax returns are selected by chance for indepth examinations which are far more exhaustive (and exhausting) than ordinary audits. The purpose is to obtain data for the Service on such items as where errors are most likely to be made by taxpayers, what instructions or forms are most likely to be misunderstood, and what requirements are especially difficult for taxpayers to meet. One person objected to being put through the wringer on a laborious item-by-item basis, claiming that I.R.S. was authorized to subject him to audit only for the purpose of seeing whether his tax liability had been reported correctly and not to accumulate statistics for a research program. But he had to submit to the same detailed scrutiny as a proven tax cheater. The Service was verifying his tax liability, held a 1980 decision, and also was seeking to find weaknesses in the compliance system, which (hopefully) would find ways of lessening the compliance problems of taxpayers in general.

Recently the Internal Revenue Service began the use of a new method of selecting tax returns for audit. Let the Service tell this story in its own words:

"The Internal Revenue Service began using a new system—Total Positive Income (TPI)—to classify tax returns to be selected for audit. In the past, most returns audited were identified through the Discriminant Function System (DIF). Returns were sorted into categories based on adjusted gross income.

"Changes in tax laws, filing characteristics, inflation, and the proliferation of abusive tax shelters called for a more effective system than adjusted gross income. For example, under the old DIF system, if a person had $100,000 of income and $95,000 of losses, the adjusted gross income would be $5,000, causing the return to be counted in the under $10,000 returns, similar to 1040As.

"Under TPI, the system will 'remember' that the total income in the above example was really $100,000, regardless of losses, and the return would be placed in a higher-income category for audit selection and other purposes."

"Other purposes" has a properly sinister sound.

What Item on Your Return Is Most Likely to Be Incorrect?

A study prepared under the Internal Revenue Service's Taxpayer Compliance Measurement Program for tax year 1973 showed that taxpayer compliance was lowest in the case of the medical expense deduction. Next came the personal casualty and theft loss deduction. More than 64% of taxpayers in the program's sample deducted the wrong amount of casualty and theft loss, according to a 1979 *Report by the Comptroller General of the United States*.

Invitations to Be Audited

In a variety of circumstances, a taxpayer is in effect asking to have his federal income tax return audited by the Internal Revenue Service.

1.   He files a claim for refund for a previous year which has not yet been closed by the statute of limitations. The return for which this claim is filed will have to be looked at by the Service to see whether the refund should be granted. The I.R.S. is no more anxious to disgorge money than is anybody else, and a review of this prior period return may not only reveal something improper which is large enough to cancel out the refund claim but something very considerably larger. Quite possibly, the refund claim can result in a tax deficiency which otherwise never would have been brought to light. This discourages many people from filing small claims, even if they appear to be completely justified. On the other hand, a refund claim may be too large to ignore.

2.   A crosscheck with information supplied to the Internal Revenue Service by other sources may result in an audit. Typically, a bank reports to the Service on an information return, Form 1099, that a certain amount of interest for a taxable year has been paid to a named taxpayer, Social Security account number so-and-so. If this item does not show up on the taxpayer's federal income tax return, someone is going to want to know why. Often the taxpayer will receive a letter asking whether the interest was reported, and the matter can be settled by correspondence. On the other hand, one item of "overlooked" income can suggest that there may be others, which only an audit can bring to light. When you receive copies of information returns which payors have sent to the Service, check them carefully against the figures which you intend to show on your income tax return. Reconcile these differences before filing your return. The Service is just about certain to note any discrepancy in reported figures.

3.   The taxpayer has employed a professional tax return preparer of dubious reliability—or worse. If the Internal Revenue Service already has tabbed this preparer as a person who is incompetent or dishonest, returns of all parties he has prepared will be examined critically by the Service in the belief than *any* returns he has prepared require adjustment.

4.   If there are questions on the income tax return which the taxpayer has not answered, a computer will flag that return for further attention. The questions were printed on the form for a definite purpose. For ex-

ample, the form asks this question: "Did you deduct expenses for an office in your home?" An answer is required. If there is nothing to be said in response to a particular question, insert "None" or "Not applicable." It is said that nature abhors a vacuum. So does the Internal Revenue Service. Failure to respond to a tax return form question will be given a sinister interpretation.

The fact that questions as to valuation of inventories were not answered on a businessperson's return, declared the Internal Revenue Service, will be considered in the Service's selection of tax returns for examination.

5. A person who has established a reputation of being a "wise guy" or a troublemaker cannot expect to be bypassed by the I.R.S. For example, an individual may derive a substantial measure of satisfaction by announcing to reporters or shouting at a tax protest meeting that he doesn't believe in paying taxes and, perhaps for sincerely cherished beliefs, refuses to do so. Some parties even have written of their defiance in books and pamphlets. Sooner or later, the Service finds it necessary to disabuse a rebellious party of his notion that he rather than the law decides what goes on his tax return. Taxpayers (or rather, non-taxpayers) consistently have fared badly when they declined to pay taxes which would be used to wage war or have objected to being taxed upon income which had been in the form of paper money rather than gold or silver. Claiming a million dependents, as one taxpayer did, is another invitation to a tax audit, for the claim did seem to be an exaggeration requiring an investigation.

In a number of situations, people have asked the courts to prevent "harassment" by the Internal Revenue Service, which allegedly had taken place because their tax returns had been selected for audit. But inasmuch as many tax returns are chosen for audit by random selection, persons who have been very critical of the I.R.S. or who have defended unpopular causes have been singularly unsuccessful in convincing a court that the fact that *their* numbers came up for audit was anything but coincidental.

A person who had proclaimed prominently that he wouldn't pay his income taxes was subjected to Internal Revenue Service audit. He claimed that he was being deprived of his right of free speech and that his return had been tabbed for audit because of his dissident views, which, he said, was illegal persecution. But in a 1979 decision, a court refused to interfere, saying that the Service cannot possibly investigate every violation of the tax laws. But if a person publicly announces that he doesn't pay his taxes, the I.R.S. can check out that statement. He had received a tax deficiency notice, not because of his loud defiance of The System, but because he owed taxes.

One individual claimed that his income tax return had been given The Eye because he was suspected of another offense which the government felt it could not prove at the time. In a 1980 decision, a court again declined to interfere. Where the government lacks the resources to prosecute every suspected wrongdoer, it is logical to give top priority to a person who is suspected of both tax and non-tax offenses.

Free speech, of course, is one of the Constitution's most treasured rights. But it can invite a legitimate tax audit. One person sought to prevent the I.R.S. from prosecuting him for failure to file income tax returns on the ground that he had been subjected to selective prosecution in violation of his right of free speech. Admittedly, he had boasted publicly of not filing tax returns because of disapproval of government spending for war and other "immoral" purposes. But, held the court, selective prosecution is banned only for impermissible grounds. Here the Service was held to have been justified in going after people who boasted of failing to obey the tax laws in order to alert taxpayers in general to the consequences of noncompliance.

It can be very helpful if you are able to find out why you are being audited by the I.R.S. One individual's income tax return was selected for audit because he was an attorney engaged in bringing damage suits for clients against insurance companies. The return of virtually every lawyer who brought suits against insurance companies in the Philadelphia area was selected after someone closely identified with that city's insurance industry had supplied leads to the I.R.S. about supposedly irregular transactions. The court refused to issue summonses ordering the taxpayers to release information to the I.R.S. on the ground that there was no evidence that they had violated any *tax* laws, the Service's proper field of investigation. I.R.S., declared the court in one decision, willingly had let itself be used as a cat's paw by the insurance industry and had not taken this action against the taxpayers for tax reasons.

Ordinarily, an angry taxpayer will be told that a computer randomly selected his return for audit and hence there has been no discrimination. But when the person chosen for audit was a career official of the American Civil Liberties Union, which frequently defended unpopular causes, he was entitled to know why his return had been plucked from the pack in order to establish whether he indeed was being harassed and punished for his zealous outspokenness.

22

6. The taxpayer has deducted, without explanation, some item which needs substantiation, such as a substantial casualty loss. If you leave it to the Service to question the item (and it will), an I.R.S. person will think of other questions to ask at the same time which you may be in a less satisfactory position to answer. Beware of using ''Miscellaneous'' or ''Sundry'' to describe anything meaningful which must be detailed.

7. If you deducted the same item on the tax returns of two different years, mention this fact on both returns. There may have been honest doubt as to the year in which to claim a deduction, and even I.R.S. employees sometimes advise in the case of genuine uncertainty to deduct the item in each year, so that eventually you will get it in the proper year. But you are not entitled to deduct the same item more than once, and if you do so, this could be regarded as fraud unless properly explained in advance. The Service has been known to zero in on deduction of the same contribution in each of two taxable years.

8. A taxpayer may fail to use the same figure on the tax return and on a schedule supporting that item in detail. For example, contributions or moving expenses may be shown at a certain amount in one place and at a different amount somewhere else on the same tax return. This is going to call for an explanation.

9. The filing of a sloppy tax return may trigger an investigation. You are not being graded on penmanship, of course. But a slovenly tax return form suggests a slovenly set of records and a slovenly taxpayer. Overlooked items frequently are discovered on such a return, which implies inattention or indifference.

10. Underpayment of taxes may arouse the suspicion of the Internal Revenue Service. Overpayment of your taxes lengthens the odds against audit. According to a report issued by the Comptroller General of the United States, *How the Internal Revenue Service Selects Individual Income Tax Returns for Audit,* persons who overpay their federal income tax returns are not so likely to be audited as persons who underpay.

11. Claiming the maximum deductions taken by persons in your income bracket invites scrutiny. Several publishers of commercial tax services have prepared their own analyses of Internal Revenue Service statistics to reveal how much the *average* taxpayer in various income brackets has deducted in the preceding year for items such as medical expenses, contributions, and the like. There is a great temptation to think that if you deduct slightly less than does the average person in your bracket, say, the $25–$30,000 range, the I.R.S. computers won't tag you as a person who seems to be padding his contributions, etc. True, the

23

computers are programmed to flag for further investigation any deduction which appears to be excessive in terms of the taxpayer's income. But one of the world's best-kept secrets is what the percentages are which the I.R.S. regards as acceptable. When one consistently skates too close to the edge, he is apt to topple over.

12. If tax deductions are itemized, there is a greater chance that the federal income tax return will be audited than if the zero-bracket amount is used. The latter takes into account a specified figure which is based upon a taxpayer's filing status (single, married–filing jointly, etc.) without regard to his income. But this is of practical use only in the case of persons with modest income. Some people deliberately fail to claim legitimate deductions on the theory that audit of something which is easily justifiable can avoid problems which could trigger big tax trouble.

13. Use of round-number figures on your tax return may interest the I.R.S. You properly may eliminate cents if you desire. But listing casualty losses, medical expenses, and the like as an even $2,000 will arouse suspicion that you got this figure out of thin air. Life isn't that neat and orderly.

14. The larger the amount of adjusted gross income on an income tax return, the greater is the likelihood that the return will be selected for examination. This is not because the Internal Revenue Service is prejudiced against wealthy persons. But experience has shown that as one's income rises, there is more opportunity to make mistakes, because forms of income and of expenditure increase. As one's income mounts, there is greater temptation to find some offsets to keep taxes from becoming too "confiscatory." You may be more eager to listen to questionable advice, to take chances, or to seek so-called tax shelters which are not so foolproof as their promoters have been claiming.

15. Computational errors can be minimized, although not eliminated, if you let the Internal Revenue Service compute your tax for you where this is possible. Taking into account all of the credits, allowances, etc., to which you are entitled can involve mistakes, especially if you are not familiar with the procedures. The necessity of using the proper tables or tax return lines and of accurately accounting for prior years' tax overpayments or amounts of employer withholding understandably can lead to errors. If you desire, the I.R.S. will compute your tax for you where adjusted gross income is $20,000 or less ($40,000 in the case of a married person filing a joint return or a qualifying widow[er]). To be eligible for this service by the Service, all of your income must be from wages, salaries, tips, dividends, interest, pensions, and annuities. You may not

use this device if you itemize your deductions in excess of the zero-bracket amount, if you average your income where there have been substantial fluctuations in recent years, or where you claim an exemption for income earned abroad. But even if you let the I.R.S. compute your income tax for you, it is a prudent idea to check the computation yourself.

16. When a taxpayer volunteers any information to the Internal Revenue Service, he may be going out of his way to invite an audit. You should answer all questions raised by the Service. But as anyone who has served in the Armed Forces has learned, never volunteer. Specifically, a taxpayer may be asked by the I.R.S., probably in the form of a letter, about some item on the tax return. Should the taxpayer reply, as many do, "That's the way I've always handled it," he is inviting scrutiny of all of his tax returns which are not yet closed by the statute of limitations. If an item is not likely to stand up to the hard critical stare of the Service this year, the worst thing you can do is to involve your tax returns of prior years which otherwise might never have been subjected to scrutiny in this specific area.

A businessperson argued that a certain form of travel expense could not be disallowed by a Revenue Agent because the Agent who had performed a previous audit stated that it was proper. A 1980 decision held that the Service can challenge claimed deductions involving inconsistent action by several Revenue Agents.

One case involved a taxpayer who wrote to the Internal Revenue Service to ask whether his accountant had paid taxes for the two preceding years, the books not being clear as to this. When he was informed that these taxes had not been transmitted, he paid them. Then he was assessed for penalty and interest on these unpaid taxes. That was too much for the court to swallow. "This case is a classic example of why the Internal Revenue Service enjoys such low repute," declared the judge who heard the taxpayer's appeal. "It also illustrates why persons who start out as willing and cooperative taxpayers end up as tax avoiders. [He] initiated the entire unbelievable procedure by voluntarily inquiring of the IRS" if certain taxes were due. Apparently the Service would not have known of these two years' unpaid taxes if he had not brought the matter to its attention. The tax was due but, concluded the court, the I.R.S. knew he was not liable for penalties and interest under the circumstances, and the rejection of his refund claim for their recovery on a mere technicality was, to the judge, "the ultimate absurdity in this bizarre episode."

17. If you choose to remain silent, the Internal Revenue Service predictably will try to find out why. A group manager of the I.R.S. Intelli-

gence Division testified in a 1979 case that a Fifth Amendment claim of the right to be silent during a routine income tax examination could possibly generate an investigation. And that isn't a bit routine.

Some Other Methods by Which Your Return May Be Tagged

If the Internal Revenue Service is seeking to determine a taxpayer's correct liability, anyone in possession of relevant records kept in the ordinary course of business can be required to show them to the Service. A taxpayer can ask a court to prevent this only if he is able to show that the information was to be used for an improper purpose, such as for use solely in a criminal investigation. That was not the situation in a 1979 case where the taxpayer had not yet been reported to enforcement officials for criminal prosecution and might never be.

Big Brother is going to know more about your cash transactions under new rules which went into effect in 1980. Banks and other financial institutions are subject to modified rules governing the reports which they must file on their individual customers' currency transactions in excess of $10,000. The report must be filed with the Service within fifteen days after the transaction. If you want to know what the government is now being told, ask your banker to show you a copy of Form 4789, *revised,* "Currency Transactions Report."

Your accountant may have to tell the I.R.S. certain things about you which you wouldn't reveal. When the Service notified one person that his tax returns were to be examined, he turned his books over to an accountant he had engaged to represent him in the audit. The accountant was not given a signed power of attorney to represent the taxpayer before the I.R.S. A Revenue Agent examined the books at the accountant's office and as a result of what he found (or didn't find), he assessed a tax deficiency. You can't use the results of your examination against me, cried the taxpayer, for that information was obtained by illegal search or seizure; I never authorized the accountant to show you anything. But you made him your agent for purposes of the audit, declared the court. If you didn't want him to show the Service anything without your approval, you should have told him so.

When the income tax return of a closely held corporation is examined by Revenue Agents, this frequently leads to an examination of the personal returns of the principal stockholders. The reason is that often there are transactions between corporations and shareholders which are at less than arm's length. Entertainment or other bills paid by a corporation on behalf of an officer-stockholder frequently are treated as being the equivalent of taxable dividends to these persons.

An executive may be entangled by a tax audit of the corporation for which he works. For example, if the company is suspected of participating in the making of illegal bribes and kickbacks, the I.R.S. has announced, that may call for "examining corporate officers' individual tax returns at the same time as the corporation's return is being examined . . ."

In the case of major corporations, there is apt to be an audit under the Coordinated Examination Program (CEP). Usually this is performed by a group of specialists as a team, and officers or principal stockholders are likely to be covered by the inquiry.

A partnership does not pay a federal income tax. But a partnership income tax return must be filed, this being a mere information return, with itemization of each type of income to every partner individually. Predictably, audit of the partnership return will be accompanied by examination of the tax returns of each partner as an individual. In the past, some partnerships omitted to file returns, as a result of which the I.R.S. was not alerted to partnership income properly reportable by each partner. The Revenue Act of 1978 imposed a new penalty upon partnerships which fail to file a completed partnership information return on time. Although this penalty is assessed against the partnership, partners are liable individually for the penalty to the extent of their liabilities for partnership debts generally.

When a person dies, a federal estate tax return has to be filed where the estate assets exceed certain stipulated amounts. Even if the estate assets seem to be too small to call for the filing of the return, the Internal Revenue Service, has the right to establish this fact for itself.

Don't let your tax records die with your spouse. When one person's federal income tax return was examined, he was unable to substantiate a number of deductions he had claimed. After he had filed the return, his wife died. His daughters, doubtless trying to be helpful in tidying up the house, swept out all of his records, including some deductions.

When a person was arrested in connection with a traffic offense, the police examined the interior of his car and found a sizeable amount of cash. A 1980 decision held that the cash could be taxed as previously unreported income.

An anti-highjacking pat-down search at an airport revealed that one passenger was carrying $20,000 in hundred-dollar bills. This was duly noted on a Customs Service currency transaction form, which was passed along to the I.R.S. A tax investigation immediately followed. The passenger claimed that his constitutional freedom from unreasonable search had been violated, and admitted the Internal Revenue Service would have known nothing about this caper except for the pat-down. But the evidence thus obtained could be used against him. He had acquiesced in the search by getting in line to board the plane. When he saw that the anti-highjacking procedure would involve a pat-down, he could have decided not to emplane, in which event he would not have been frisked.

Customarily, the estate tax examiner will call for all federal income tax returns for the last three years of the decedent's life, to see, for example, whether there had been any transactions within three years of death which automatically would require the inclusion of transferred assets in the decedent's gross estate. Although different I.R.S. personnel are involved in income and in estate tax examinations, the estate tax examiner is required to bring in the income tax examiners in appropriate circumstances.

One never knows what circumstances have led Revenue Agents to his door. An off-duty Revenue Agent was displeased by the service he had received at a bar. He instituted an "independent pickup" or requisition of the proprietor's federal income tax returns, which resulted in the discovery of tax deficiencies and an allegation of fraud.

Revenue Agents, through their own alertness, may be attracted to a taxable situation. The tax law provides that the Secretary of the Treasury, to the extent that he considers it practicable, may direct tax people "to proceed, from time to time through each internal revenue district and inquire after and concerning all persons therein who may be liable to pay an internal revenue tax, and all persons owning or having the care and management of any objects with respect to which any tax is imposed." It was through observant Revenue Agents in the streets that a "cash only" merchant was apprehended in a 1979 case.

When a contractor refused to hire union labor, a union representative declared that the contractor could expect an official visit by a Revenue Agent. Sure enough, that's just what happened.

Newspapers printed the story of how a nine-year-old boy was apprehended by the state police while driving his father's car at seventy-five miles per hour on the Garden State Parkway. He was eloping with the seven-year-old girl who lived next door, said the article, and he had with him $5,000 in cash which he had taken from the desk drawer of his father, a well-known physician. Concluded the article, "The Internal Revenue Service has expressed great interest in his story."

Individuals sometimes write to the Internal Revenue Service headquarters in Washington for a ruling on the income tax aspects of a transaction. Copies of the I.R.S. ruling are sent to the Service office where the taxpayer files his returns, so that the ruling is available when the tax return is examined.

Although by law a person's federal income tax return is confidential between him and the Internal Revenue Service, there is an interchange of "interesting" information between the Service and various governmental enforcement agencies, such as the Department of Justice, the Federal Trade Commission, and the Federal Bureau of Investigation. The I.R.S. also has "treaties" with state tax departments for the exchange of information.

The I.R.S. cannot use against you any information it has obtained by illegal wiretapping. But if another governmental agency has gotten a court order to wiretap for its own purposes, the juicy tidbits can be turned over to the Service, which then has the right, declared a 1981 decision, to use the information which it had not obtained illegally.

It is easy to cut down on one's federal income tax withholding by overstating the number of dependents on Form W–4, "Employee's Withholding Exemption Certificate," which must be provided to the employer. But the days of big families, for tax reporting purposes, may be coming to an end. Starting in 1980, employers must send to the Internal Revenue Service copies of all such certificates listing ten or more withholding allowance claims. It will take a real stork to outrace the Service computers.

The Internal Revenue Service has a training manual and a special school on tax shelters. In consequence any Revenue Agent, however unfamiliar he may be with the intricacies and sophistication of some tax shelters, can plug into the resources of highly trained specialists in this area.

Not all tax shelters are abusive, and yours may withstand any scrutiny by the Internal Revenue Service. But can you say the same for *every* other item on the return which has been selected for probing by a suspicious examiner?

In one 1980 case, the I.R.S. had sought to ascertain the correct federal income tax liabilities of all persons who had purchased rights to certain "master recordings" promoted by a corporation that sold such rights, As there was a likelihood of unpaid taxes by the investors if this were indeed what the Service calls an "abusive tax shelter," the company had to reveal names, addresses, and Social Security numbers of all investors. Even if a particular venture turns out to be one hundred percent clean, legal and ethical, the I.R.S. has a right to see for itself how investors are reporting the transaction.

The Tax Informant

Your federal income tax return may be singled out for audit because of information which the Internal Revenue Service receives that suggests that the return is not complete or that it is downright dishonest. The subject will be considered in depth in Chapter 4, "What Big Brother Already Knows About You." Let it suffice at this point to note that anyone's tax return will be scrutinized carefully if the I.R.S. thinks the time expended for a massive application of manpower will be justified in terms of additional tax, penalty, and interest to be collected. If someone "snitches" on a taxpayer in such areas as unreported income or unjustified deductions, and the information appears to be credible, a suspect tax return will be checked out carefully.

An accounting firm noted in its certification of a business's financial statement that "we were not able to examine the Company's sales and accounts receivable under generally accepted auditing standards. Because of the above limitations on the scope of our examinations we were unable to express an opinion as to whether the accompanying financial statements present fairly either the financial position of [the business] . . . or the results of its operations and changes in financial position for the year then ended." Whether the I.R.S. actually was alerted to shortcoming in the business's records by this statement, or whether there was a deliberate leak, no one said. Revenue Agents do look at everything which may help them to do their job. Here the Service established, to its own satisfaction and the court's, its right to reconstruct income other than by the business's books, which had been discovered somehow to be unreliable.

The Freedom of Information Act now enables a person to learn what information the government has on him in its cavernous files in most situations. But no one has the right to see "investigatory records compiled for law enforcement purposes." So in a 1979 case, a taxpayer was not permitted to ask the source of certain information the Service was using against him. This was unsolicited information that someone had put into the I.R.S. pipeline, and to let a taxpayer know who had blown the whistle would deter other people who "know things" from telling the government about them.

Know What the I.R.S. Is Likely to Look At

If you know what a tax examiner is likely to zero in on, you will understand better how he or she can be led to a closer scrutiny of your tax returns. Under the recent Freedom of Information Act, governmental agencies now are obliged to make public various data which previously had been secret.

As a result of this Act, the following Internal Revenue Service audit handbooks have been made available to the public. They may be purchased from several commercial publishers:

Audit Technique Handbook for Internal Revenue Agents
Handbook for Special Agents
Techniques Handbook for In-Depth Audit Investigations
A Legal Reference Guide for Revenue Officers (This explains how delinquent taxes are collected.)
Audit Technique Handbook for Estate Tax Examiners.

Two Types of Revenue Agents

There are two types of Internal Revenue Agents. A taxpayer should be able to tell them apart instantly, for this will enable him to know why his tax affairs are being examined.

A *Revenue Agent* examines federal income tax returns and determines the correct tax liability. He is not authorized to investigate criminal tax fraud, and when his examination reveals the possibility of fraud, he must suspend the examination and refer the matter to the Intelligence Division of the I.R.S. for resolution of the fraud question.

When a referral is made to the Intelligence Division, a *Special Agent* is assigned to make a preliminary investigation. The primary duties of a Special Agent are the investigation of possible criminal violations of the tax law, the development of information concerning possible criminal violation of these statutes, the evaluation of such information, and the recommendation of prosecution when warranted. The duties of the Special Agent include the power to investigate and to arrest.

Revenue Agents are not required to give warning that information given by an individual can be used against him in a tax matter. Special Agents are obliged to inform taxpayers that "one of my functions is to investigate the possibility of criminal violations of the Internal Revenue laws . . ." In one case, a Special Agent visited a taxpayer at his residence but failed to give this warning. At a later meeting he did so. A court held

31

that all information given by the taxpayer at this first meeting had to be suppressed because he had not been warned of the nature of the investigation and his rights to remain silent and to have counsel present. But information the taxpayer supplied at a later meeting after he had been warned that anything he said could be used against him was properly useable by the government, for this information had not been tainted by the original failure to warn the taxpayer of what was going on.

The United States Supreme Court has said that when a taxpayer has not been warned of the right to remain silent, the right to have counsel present, and the right to have counsel appointed by the court if he was unable to hire a lawyer, the government's case against him must be dismissed, even if he was not an accused person in custody at the time as in the well-known *Miranda* case.

To avoid controversy as to whether he really had been advised of his Constitutional rights, a taxpayer, as soon as he sees from his visitor's card (by all means read it!) that he is a Special Agent, should decline to discuss even the time of day until he has competent counsel present. This is highly advisable even if the taxpayer is confident that he has nothing to hide.

Unnecessary Examination

If a taxpayer's books and records already have been examined by a Revenue Agent, a second examination may be characterized as harassment. A person properly may refuse to undergo a second examination unless the District Director of Internal Revenue approves the request on Form L-153 or by letter. Refusal by a taxpayer to permit a second examination without this formal demand in writing frequently will terminate the request by Revenue Agents for a second "go-around," for they may not want their superior officer to know why the request really had been made: for example, a Revenue Agent may have learned after his audit report had been submitted that because of ignorance of the law or carelessness, he had failed to disallow certain items. Or the Agent might be worried that if he does not correct something which he had permitted previously, this will be discovered to his embarrassment by the Revenue Agent who looks at the following year's return. Refusal of a taxpayer to agree to a second examination does not necessarily mean the end of the matter. The District Director may want to have the work of one Revenue Agent checked if there have been complaints about the quality of his performance. Or the Service may have second thoughts about how a certain type of item should be treated.

If a taxpayer objects strenuously to a second examination but permits it to begin while he checks with counsel, the examination will be permitted despite what the lawyer may say about lack of permission. Once the Revenue Agent is allowed to commence a re-examination, this is deemed to be consent to complete it.

The rule against unauthorized second examination does not apply if there never had been a complete first examination. Such is the situation when, because of illness or re-assignment of the Agent, the original examination was suspended. That also is the situation when the taxpayer had failed to supply everything which was requested in the original examination. One Revenue Agent was permitted, without written authorization from the District Director, to look at a taxpayer's records which actually had been examined previously by another Agent, who announced after his audit that he was satisfied and that the tax return would be accepted as submitted. Unfortunately for the taxpayer, the Agent left the Service before writing up the case. The original examination was deemed not to have been completed because the taxpayer had not been notified *in writing* that the return had been accepted.

Repetitive Audits

If an individual has undergone one or more audits for the two preceding taxable years which resulted in either no change of tax liability or only a small change, he may request discontinuance of the examination should it involve the same issues which had been reviewed previously. Upon receipt of this request, the examiner will review the prior file and make a determination as to whether or not the issues currently under examination are essentially similar to those which had resulted in no significant tax change. If the issues are indeed similar and no other compelling reasons exist for examining the return, the audit will be terminated and the taxpayer so notified.

Transferee Liability

An individual may be subjected to additional federal income taxes without being audited at all. This comes about when someone is required to pay another party's taxes because the former is a transferee of the person who originally owed the taxes.

If property is transferred at a time when the transferor is insolvent, or if he is made insolvent by the transfer because he has not retained sufficient assets to pay his liabilities, any unpaid federal taxes of the transferor may be collected from the transferee or transferees, up to the fair market value which each one has received. The Internal Revenue Service does not have to proceed against each person individually when there are several transferees. The Service may collect the full unpaid tax from *one* transferee if he has received enough property to pay for it; he cannot insist that the I.R.S. limit his liability to the percentage of the transferor's total property which he received. Nor has he any way of collecting from the other transferees their proportionate share of this tax. He is entitled to no form of deduction.

Transferee liability can arise in the case of gifts from individuals. A shareholder in a corporation similarly is liable for corporate taxes if the company was liquidated and such shareholder received his proportionate interest in the company's net assets, for example, if the corporation was audited after liquidation had taken place, and there were no assets remaining to pay a federal tax deficiency.

A person may have to pay additional taxes as a transferee without the opportunity of satisfying himself that these taxes were properly assessed against the transferor. Tax returns are confidential between a taxpayer and the Internal Revenue Service. Thus the transferee has no right to see the return which supposedly was the cause of the taxes he now must pay. Perhaps the original taxpayer had been correct in the first instance and no additional taxes were owed. Perhaps the I.R.S. had made a mistake, even an arithmetical one, in computing the transferee liability. The unfortunate transferee is helpless in such situations.

If transferee liability is imposed, it applies not only to the transferor's unpaid federal taxes but also to penalties resulting from these unpaid taxes, plus interest.

When transferee liability is established, the statute of limitations as far as the transferee is concerned is extended to one year beyond what it had been in the case of the transferor.

If a corporation distributes its assets to the stockholders, as when the company is liquidated, any unpaid corporate taxes may be collected from the shareholders up to the value of the property each has received. One such stockholder vainly asked a court to prevent the placing of a government lien for unpaid taxes against her own property because she had never received notice that she owed taxes as a transferee. In a 1980 decision, the court refused. The I.R.S. had sent a letter to her correct ad-

dress, or so the record indicated. Under the law, she *had* been notified—
even if really she hadn't been.

Joint Returns and the Innocent Spouse

An individual may be obliged to pay federal income taxes which are
not based upon his income; in fact, he may not even know the income
existed. If husband and wife file a joint federal income tax return, each
spouse is liable for the entire tax, not only the tax upon his or her portion
of the income. So if the husband has failed to report any of his income,
the wife is liable for the tax on it, even if he disappears with the money.
This applies to penalty and interest as well.

A spouse (here called for convenience the wife, although it could be
either party) will not be liable for tax on income unreported by her husband if all of these three conditions apply: (1) there was an omission of
gross income in excess of 25%, (2) the wife proves she had not known of
the omission and had no reason to know of it, and (3) she did not benefit
significantly from the unreported income.

If the family had been spending at a rate in excess of her income and
what the husband reported, it is difficult for the wife to argue that she had
not known of unreported income or at least had no reason to know of it.
In addition, she might have benefitted significantly from it, for example,
if she had received lavish gifts of jewelry and furs. An allegedly innocent
spouse cannot close her eyes to unusual or extravagant expenditures. She
has the burden of proving that she was unaware of the unreported income.

When one man with a modest salary had substantial income from gambling which he reported neither to the I.R.S. nor to his wife, the I.R.S.
claimed that she also was responsible for tax on this revenue omitted from
the joint tax return. She must have known of his gambling income, argued the government. But in a 1980 decision, the court felt otherwise
because the European-born husband, when asked whether he had discussed his income with his wife, replied that "under the . . . custom [of
our country], we have a way of not telling our wives anything. We don't
want to hurt them, we don't want to cheapen them."

In a 1980 case, the Internal Revenue Service argued that the wife
couldn't avoid tax liability as an innocent spouse because, still being
married to the perpetrator, she still *might* profit from the unreported income although she had not as yet. *Might* doesn't count for this purpose,
it was ruled, for "the statute does not limit its benefits to spouses who are
deserted, divorced, or separated."

3.
Nobody Is Going to Take Your Word for It

A taxpayer has to do more than pay taxes. He also has the burden of keeping records to show why he should not be paying more taxes.

In this country, we are justifiably proud of the fact that a person is innocent until proven guilty. In federal tax matters, however, that rule is applied the other way around. A person is guilty (taxable) unless he can prove that what comes in, or what he has, does not represent taxable income. But nothing is deductible on his federal income tax return unless he can prove his right to take that deduction. Except in a few areas which most taxpayers never meet, but which will be listed later in this chapter, the burden of proof always is upon the taxpayer. Subject to these few identified exceptions, anything which the Internal Revenue Service says will stand unless the taxpayer can prove that *his* point of view is correct. The taxpayer must, in the words of Gilbert and Sullivan's *The Mikado*, provide "corroborative detail and artistic verisimilitude to an otherwise bald and unconvincing narrative."

In actual practice, the Internal Revenue Service makes a "finding" as to taxability or non-deductibility. This finding is presumed by law to be correct, unless the taxpayer can refute it.

Although a person has the *legal* right to remain silent, that is not enough in a tax matter. By remaining silent, a taxpayer is not refuting a finding of the Internal Revenue Service. Despite the guarantee of the United States Constitution, a taxpayer remains silent at his peril. Why a taxpayer remains silent instead of offering proof of his position is deemed to be irrelevant. In one case, a taxpayer's husband vainly argued that his wife had refused to dispute a Revenue Agent's disallowances on her federal income tax because she "was excessively afraid of the Internal Revenue Service."

The taxpayer's burden of proof extends to everything which appears on his tax return, or which the Internal Revenue Service says should have appeared there.

Difficulty of Proof Is No Defense

There is an ancient saying that the law doesn't require the impossible. Frequently this does not seem to apply in federal income tax matters. A taxpayer unquestionably has been robbed of a valuable piece of jewelry. Loss deduction depends upon the establishment of the tax basis of the property in her hands, which, in the case of a gift, is what the donor paid for the property. But the taxpayer does not know what the donor paid for it; it's considered rude to ask anyone how much he paid for a present. Now the donor is dead, and no one knows what happened to his records or even if he had kept any. No one even knows who the dealer was or when the purchase took place. But in order to get a tax deduction for the stolen property, the person whose jewelry was taken somehow must prove the donor's cost.

Expenses of, or losses from, a transaction entered upon for profit are deductible. An individual collects postage stamps, and he seeks to deduct related expenses such as insurance and travel costs to buy at auction sales. As far as most people are concerned, the collection of stamps is a hobby, a personal matter, and expenses are not tax-deductible. This individual has the problem of proving, somehow, that although he was engaged in another business or profession, he also was in the stamp business. He must show that he bought stamps primarily for the purpose of making a profit, even if he truly enjoyed looking at the stamps. He will win his tax deduction only if he can show that his primary purpose was the expectation of making a profit. This he will try to do by showing that he engaged knowledgeable professionals to advise him what stamps had the greatest possibility of market appreciation, that he kept businesslike records of purchases and sales, that an accountant regularly reported to him about his profit and loss statement, that the collection was insured and safeguarded in the manner of valuable business inventory, that he subscribed to professional publications, that he advertised his wares. In other words, he has to prove that stamp collecting was not primarily for his personal pleasure.

A salesman uses his own car frequently in connection with his business activities. In order to get a tax deduction for the vehicle's maintenance and operating expenses when the car is used for business purposes, he must prove the extent to which the car has been used for business as opposed to personal purposes. If he cannot prove the extent to which his own car has been used for business purposes, all expenses will be deemed to be personal, non-deductible.

A difficult form of proof is the establishment of gambling losses. Gambling losses are not themselves deductible, but they may be used as an offset to gambling gains, which are taxable. Race tracks and other operators of establishments where gambling is conducted are required to report to the Internal Revenue Service all moneys earned by an individual in excess of a very modest amount. So the I.R.S. already knows what your gambling income is. But the tracks do not report your losses. You have to establish that figure in a believable manner. Bets and wagers usually are made in cash; you have no cancelled checks. You may have a box full of tickets for horses or dogs that never came in, but the existence of these pieces of paper is not proof that *you* lost the money. It's all too easy to pick unsuccessful tickets off the turf to which they have been flung by disgusted bettors immediately after a race. On the other hand, the courts will be apt to be sympathetic if you show a string of "losing" tickets which have consecutive serial numbers, such as a single bettor might have purchased. It is not unlikely that you would have been able to assemble a collection of consecutive numbers from discards. You could have a witness to testify that he actually saw you place X number of dollars at the pari-mutuel windows on unsuccessful animals. But not all racetrack characters are regarded as credible witnesses in court.

If a racetrack reports to the Internal Revenue Service that you won a specified amount on a named date, when as a matter of fact you did not, this will be treated as taxable income unless you can prove that you didn't win that money. Proving that you did not get a cash payout is a tough assignment. But, as mentioned earlier, any I.R.S. finding is presumed to be correct unless you can prove otherwise.

Medical expenses are deductible to the extent that, in total, they exceed 3% of a person's adjusted gross income for that year. Frequently it is difficult if not impossible to prove whether the primary purpose of an expenditure was medical, such as is required to get the deduction. If an individual has a nose job performed, this may have been done for the purpose of correcting a breathing impairment and unquestionably is a proper medical expense deduction. But the work may have been done for reasons of vanity, which means the expense is personal, non-deductible. Both factors may have been involved to some extent: a person's breath intake may have been improved, but so was his physical appearance. He must prove what the primary purpose was in a situation of this sort.

Frequently an individual expects to be able to prove some fact to the satisfaction of the Internal Revenue Service, if necessary, by calling upon the testimony or evidence of some thoroughly believable person who is knowledgeable about all of the necessary details. Reliance upon an individual rather than upon records is dangerous, for by the time the Service asks questions, he may be dead or senile or just plain unavailable. In one case, a court quoted sadly from the writings of Robert Ingersoll, "From the voiceless lips of the unreplying dead there comes no word."

One businessperson claimed bad debt deductions for uncollectible sales. When pressed by the Internal Revenue Service for specific names and figures, he claimed that all of the records had been taken by the bookkeeper who had been discharged at about the time that the tax audit began. Without details as to the debtors and the unpaid amounts, the court would not allow a deduction. Why, asked His Honor unrealistically, had none of the alleged debtors stepped forward to admit what still was owed?

What Happens When You Have No Proof

If a taxpayer has no proof of a claimed deduction, the Internal Revenue Service can disallow the item entirely. The taxpayer is not exactly being characterized as a liar; he merely had failed to meet his burden of proof. But all is not necessarily lost. An important case in this area involved the celebrated actor George M. Cohan, who undeniably had heavy legitimate expenses for entertainment related to his business; unfortunately, he had no records, receipts, or other substantiation of specific expenses. Under what has become known as the "Cohan rule," it was held that if a taxpayer unquestionably has expenditures of a specific nature which would be deductible, except for the lack of documentation, a court, if it chooses, can arrive at its own figure of the amount allowable, bearing down heavily against the taxpayer because the inexactitude is of his own making. Under the "Cohan rule," courts have determined amounts to be allowed as deductions in the area of unsubstantiated charitable contributions, medical expenses, casualty losses, business repairs, gambling losses. Usually the deduction permitted under this rule is far less than the taxpayer had claimed. But at least *some* deduction is permitted, if the court chooses, although a taxpayer actually is entitled to nothing without substantiation.

Lost substantiation for one year may be accepted by a court because of excellent records for the preceding year. An individual's gambling records for 1975 were lost when he changed his residence. But he produced his 1974 records: notations on racing programs of how much he had placed on various horses and the amounts he received back, with notations each day in a spiral notebook which were summarized on a schedule attached to his 1974 Federal income tax return. Winnings shown on his schedule were the same as what had been reported by the tracetracks on 1099 forms. His 1975 return had a comparable schedule, although without the lost back-up substantiation. The court in a 1980 decision allowed the total losses he had claimed for 1975, believing that that year's returns must have been as accurate as his painstaking records for the previous year.

Travel and Entertainment Expenses

Business travel and entertainment expenses may constitute proper tax deductions. But the rules here are much tougher than in the case of other deductions.

First of all, the "Cohan rule" does not apply to business travel, business entertainment, and business gifts. The Internal Revenue Service is not authorized to allow one cent of deduction for these items which is not completely substantiated. The most credible estimates will not be acceptable.

Second, there is a specific set of substantiation requirements for these items which is not required elsewhere. There must be *contemporary* recording of who was entertained, when, where, how much was spent, the relationship of the person(s) entertained to the taxpayer's trade or business, and the *business reason* for the expenditure. In addition, payments are disallowed to the extent that they are extravagant or lavish. This detailed documentation is not required for expenditures not exceeding $25, if the fact of the entertainment and the names of the person(s) involved is entered in a diary at the time of the expenditure.

These requirements, in actual practice, may be more difficult to meet than the mere words suggest. For example, in a case in which a businessperson entered details of Saturday night's entertainment in a diary when he got back to the office on Monday, it was ruled that the deduction was unallowable because of failure to make a record contemporaneously.

Destruction or Loss of Records

If the records that a taxpayer would use to substantiate tax return deductions are not available, under proper circumstances the taxpayer has the opportunity to reconstruct these records from whatever sources are available. The taxpayer must establish that his failure to produce records is because of their loss under circumstances beyond his control, such as destruction by fire, flood, earthquake, or other casualty. Only then is a reasonable reconstruction of records permitted to serve as substantiation for a claimed deduction. Admittedly, a taxpayer has a difficult problem here. Even if his records were destroyed in a fire, he has to convince the Internal Revenue Service or a court that the destroyed records actually had contained substantiation of an acceptable type; mere destruction of records does not imply that there had been acceptable proof there. When a car in which a person's records allegedly were located was stolen, he has the burden of showing that acceptable supporting papers actually were in the car at that time. He must show that the loss was not because of his own negligence. And he must establish that a casualty had been responsible for the absence of records. In the words of one decision, "The mere loss or misplacement of records does not sufficiently resemble flood or fire to be considered a casualty."

Photography and the Burden of Proof

Often a taxpayer can meet his burden of proof with photographs, if he or someone else had enough awareness of the tax significance to take pictures at the right time. Instances are:

1. The extent of casualty damage, such as a picture of the taxpayer's house immediately after a large tree had crashed through the roof.

2. Pictures of the taxpayer and persons he had entertained at a restaurant or club, properly identified so as to establish the business relationship of the expenditure.

3. A taxpayer can deduct the cost of special clothing or uniforms only if they are not properly useable for street or social purposes. Pictures can establish the specialized nature of this garb. For example, a company's trade name may be prominently displayed on a jacket.

4. A business repair is deductible if it is a mere replacement of something which has broken or worn out, and it does not constitute an improvement of the property. "Before and after" photographs can establish what actually was involved in the expenditure.

5. Certain losses from theft are deductible. A photograph may show that the lock on a door had been demolished forcibly.

6. When property is added to one's home for medical purposes and this property has a useful life of more than one year, the expenditure is not deductible, unless it can be demonstrated that the value of the home was not increased. On the basis of photographs, one court decided that

an elevator installation in the home of a victim of hypertrophic arthritis did not constitute an improvement of the premises from the standpoint of appearance. So the full cost was deductible.

But a taxpayer's use of photographs can boomerang into a fraud charge. A physician claimed a deduction for a portion of the maintenance costs of his home, alleging that in addition to his regular office at a different location, he also practiced medicine at home and saw patients there. He showed the Revenue Agent a photograph of a room in his home which was said to be used as a treatment facility for patients. Visible in the picture was a refrigerator, the open door of which revealed an imposing row of medicine bottles. But by use of a powerful magnifying glass, the Revenue Agent was able to read the labels, which showed the contents were veterinary medicines. And as a personal hobby, the doctor had some horses stabled near his home. The court refused to accept as convincing the explanation by the physician that he sometimes administered animal medicines to his human patients.

Casualty Losses

A casualty loss is deductible, although in the case of personal as opposed to business property, the first $100 of each such loss is not an allowable deduction. A major problem in obtaining this deduction is proof. Casualty losses such as from fire, flood, earthquake, blight, and the like must be shown to have been sudden. But if a boiler bursts, the taxpayer must prove that this was not the result of gradual deterioration or weakening of the walls over a period of time, for the necessary element of suddenness is missing here. Although losses occasioned by ordinary negligence are deductible, those brought about by gross negligence do not qualify as casualty losses. Such is the case where an accident was caused by drunken driving, which is characterized as gross negligence; loss caused by careless driving by an inexperienced person on an icy road is deductible as ordinary negligence. Most casualty losses are deductible only in the taxable year of occurrence, and the taxpayer must establish this by showing the occurrence of an identifiable event.

A casualty loss deduction requires that the property be destroyed or damaged by a casualty. If you don't know how the damage occurred, you have not proven that there was a casualty loss. Cracks were found in a concrete building after construction blasting had taken place in the neighborhood. But no casualty loss was proven, for faulty workmanship might have led to the formation of the cracks. A building or roof collapse because of improper design is not regarded as a casualty loss for tax purposes. If a vehicle which had been purchased in used condition should fall apart on the highway, the owner must prove *why*. There could have been an accident, which usually qualifies as a casualty. On the other hand, the vehicle, because of improper maintenance in the past or metal fatigue, may have been wasting away for years until eventually it disintegrated. This lacks the element of suddenness required for a casualty loss deduction. The owner of the property must prove what happened.

In the case of theft losses, the problem is establishment of the fact that property actually was taken without the owner's consent. If the property merely is missing, there is no proof that a theft occurred. Perhaps the owner was careless and forgot where he left the property. Perhaps he loaned it to someone else.

To establish that a theft loss actually has taken place, the owner of property should immediately report the happening to the police. Otherwise he may be deemed not to have considered what took place a theft until, at some later time, this was suggested by the person who prepared his tax return. If the perpetrator is apprehended, the property owner has to prosecute, or he may be considered to have given the property away, as where an employer felt sorry for a lifelong employee who had stolen because of the great pressure of a financial emergency. A loss is not recognized for tax purposes if reimbursement was possible from an insurance company or other party, because here the loss actually is another party's. For example, property is stolen. It is insured, but the owner, with some justification, feels that if he files a claim with his insurance company (especially if he has filed a previous claim in the not too distant past), the insurance company will cancel his policy or will fail to renew it when it expires. Rather than face the loss of insurance coverage, the property owner decides not to file a claim with his insurance company. Instead, he claims a casualty loss deduction on his federal income tax return. The Internal Revenue Service predictably will disallow it, because he could have gotten reimbursement, and therefore it was not his loss.

A theft loss deduction is allowed where the owner of money or other property voluntarily gave it to someone else because of misrepresentation, if what took place was defined as a crime under the law of the state where the event occurred. In some states, there is a theft if property is taken away through misrepresentation. In other states, to be a theft, the misrepresentation must have been made with deliberate intent to appropriate the victim's property for the taker's own purpose. Here the victim must prove what the taker's intent had been, although this may be established by circumstantial evidence.

State law also decides whether there is a theft loss deduction for federal income tax purposes when one spouse steals from the other. In some states, inter-spousal theft is not recognized as a crime. Then there is no federal tax deduction, even if property has been taken and is lost forever. This problem can be complicated even further by state law. Was the marriage valid under state law when the theft took place? If not, there was no inter-spousal theft.

Employer Payments to Employee's Widow(er)

Many companies have a practice of voluntarily making payments to the spouse of an employee who dies while still on the payroll. This may be a flat dollar amount, or it may be the equivalent of wage continuance of the deceased employee for a period of time, or it may be a set percentage of the compensation which otherwise would have been earned by the decedent.

Payment for services represents ordinary taxable income, whether the payment is made to the person who provided the services or to someone else, such as his widow. To avoid tax upon the voluntary payments made by the employer, the widow must show that the payment was not made for *services*. She must establish that the payment represented something else, such as the employer's concern for the fact that her husband's untimely death had left her and her children in a very difficult financial situation. Perhaps the employer is not familiar with the tax treatment of his payment to the widow. It therefore is up to her to inform the employer that it is important for her to have the payment to be given to her by reason of her financial condition and not because of recognition by the company of her husband's fifteen years of faithful service. Why the payment actually was made depends upon the intent for the act and the ability to prove, if such is the case, that it was not for services.

If, as sometimes happens, the employer seeks to look into the widow's financial circumstances in order to learn whether a gift should be made to her upon her husband's death, she should cooperate fully. On numerous occasions, the widow indignantly refused to answer questions about her finances on the ground that this was an invasion of her privacy. She resented suggestions that her late husband had not provided for her and the children adequately, even if in fact such was the case. By making it impossible for the employer to authorize payments to her because of her financial condition, she will be taxed upon any payments she receives inasmuch as they probably represent compensation for the husband's services. Nothing to the contrary appears in the record.

Negligence

If a tax deficiency is imposed against a person, he may be subjected to a penalty for negligence. Penalty can be waived if he shows one of the following:

1. He observed reasonable care and prudence in the preparation and filing of his income tax return.

2. He relied upon the advice of a competent person to whom he had made a full disclosure of all of the facts.

3. He was a person without any training or background in taxes, and the question he mishandled was so technical that anyone without experience in the area would not even have recognized that there was a problem which should have been referred to a professional advisor.

4. He became ill or disabled shortly before the tax return was due, and this prevented him from requesting more time in which to prepare his tax return properly or to find someone else to do it for him.

Inasmuch as the Internal Revenue Service does not have to prove negligence but it does have to prove the existence of fraud, the Service frequently asserts a negligence penalty simply because of inability to meet the more serious burden. Such was the situation when a woman listed her husband on her own federal income tax return as a dependent child. (Perhaps that's what he really was.)

Negative Burden of Proof

Most facts are not too difficult to prove, if one realizes in time that he must prove them and takes the proper steps. In a number of situations, however, a taxpayer is faced with a much more difficult problem: establishment of the fact that something didn't happen. Here are the principal areas where this negative proof must be established:

1. There may have been no possibility of reimbursement from anyone which would have wiped out or at least reduced the amount of a loss.

2. In the case of a debt which was claimed to have been bad at the end of the taxable year, the taxpayer must prove that the debt was not also bad at the beginning of this year. There can be no bad debt write-off in a taxable year if the debt was worthless when the year began.

3. Cash found in a person's safe-deposit box or living room table may not represent previously unreported income. Actually the money may have represented the repayment of an old loan and not taxable income. It is difficult to prove that a cash hoard is not an accumulation of income which should have been taxed when earned.

4. If there are unexplained bank deposits or increases in net worth during the taxable period, the taxpayer somehow must show that taxable income had not gone unreported. There may have been receipt of an inheritance rather than taxable income. One man was able to show that he had been given $200,000 in cash by a woman fifty years older than he was, in return for his promise to marry her. The proof was difficult or awkward in his situation, for he had made her a promise never to tell anyone what happened monetarily. This money now was regarded as a gift to him and not taxable income, although the I.R.S. might have argued that as far as he was concerned, he indeed had earned the funds.

5. When information that a person has supplied to a Special Agent is used against him in court, he must show that he was never warned that anything he said could be used against him or told that he had a right to have counsel present.

6. When an individual reported on his tax return a loss on a sale of property to a friend, the taxpayer had to show that there had been no prior agreement that his friend would sell his property back to him in a later year at the same price.

7. When a wife claims that she should not be responsible for taxes on income which her husband had earned but which was omitted from their joint income tax return, she must prove that she had no knowledge of this unreported income and had not benefitted significantly from it.

8. When a person receives money from his employer as reimbursement for an expense account, it must be proven that this was not a form of compensation but actually represented repayment of what he had spent on company business.

9. If a tax audit reveals that income was understated, the taxpayer must show that this was not the result of intentional disregard of the laws and regulations.

10. When a business expense is properly deductible because it meets the guidelines for allowance, the taxpayer must show that the expenditure was not unreasonable in amount.

11. If a stockholder has borrowed money from a corporation, he must show that what he received was not really a disguised dividend payment. For example, he may establish that he had signed a note for a loan, on which he paid interest regularly at the going rate, and that the corporation showed his borrowing on its books as a loan.

12. If a shareholder receives a distribution from a corporation, in order to avoid tax on ordinary income he must show that the corporation had no earnings and profits at the time, for by definition, a taxable dividend is a distribution of earnings and profits.

13. If a person claims credit on his federal income tax return for a dependent, he must show that the dependent did not receive half of his support from another person.

14. When a dependent is claimed, the taxpayer must show that the dependent did not have income of more than $999.99 that year. This can present a difficult practical problem. For example, the taxpayer may claim his mother as a dependent, but she may refuse to tell him what her income is.

Where the I.R.S. Has the Burden of Proof

In almost every situation which a taxpayer encounters, the burden of proof is upon him. Here are the places where the Internal Revenue Service must shoulder the burden of proof:

1. Although a taxpayer has the burden of proof when the Internal Revenue Service makes a finding of negligence, the Service has the burden when fraud is charged. Fraud is defined as the willful evasion of taxes known to be due. Unlike the gentle 5% negligence penalty, there is a 50% fraud penalty, specific dollar fines depending upon what the fraudulent act was, and there are prison terms. In addition, where fraud is found, the statute of limitations never closes a tax return as far as the I.R.S. is concerned.

Inasmuch as fraud requires the Service to establish *willfulness*, intent to evade taxes must be shown. Actually, the government rarely even tries to show what the taxpayer had in mind. Instead, fraud is established by circumstantial evidence. Most fraud cases won by the I.R.S. hinged upon the Service's establishment of "badges of fraud," such as:

A. The taxpayer had such excellent training and experience (for example, he was a certified public accountant specializing in tax matters) that any omission of income must have been deliberate, as he must have known better. Even a person without specialized experience and formal education can be found guilty of fraud on the ground that he must have known that what he was doing was improper, as in a case in which a woman was shown to be highly knowledgeable about her business affairs.

47

B.   There had been a consistent pattern of under-reporting income, or padding expenses, over the years. This couldn't have been just coincidental.

C.   The taxpayer had destroyed his own records just before the tax audit began.

D.   The taxpayer had bank accounts in fictitious names.

E.   The taxpayer was consistently hostile and uncooperative with Revenue Agents who were trying to check the returns.

F.   The taxpayer described items in his checkbook differently from the way they were described on invoices.

2.   Where a person is assessed by way of transferee liability for the unpaid taxes of someone else, the Internal Revenue Service has to show that the transferee had received property with a fair market value at least as great as the amount assessed against him from a person who, at the time of the transfer, owed federal taxes and who was insolvent, or became insolvent as a result of the transfer.

3.   The three-year statute of limitations for tax returns is extended to six years if gross income has been understated by more than 25%. The Service must show that there has been such understatement.

4.   The Service must show that it mailed a notice of tax deficiency within the permitted time to the taxpayer's last-known address.

5.   If the I.R.S. disallows an expenditure on the ground that its allowance would be contrary to public policy, the Service must show that there is such a clearly-defined policy which is being enforced.

6.   Losses are allowed in the case of transactions entered upon for profit. If a person engages in an activity which appears to be more of a hobby than a business to him, he is presumed to be engaged in the activity for profit in the taxable year if in two or more years of a period of five consecutive years (seven, where horses are involved) ending with the current taxable year, the activity was carried on at a profit. But the Internal Revenue Service has the opportunity of showing, if it can, that despite some profit years, the activity was not intended by the taxpayer to be carried on as a business but as a hobby.

7.   Sometimes a taxpayer and the I.R.S. enter into a *closing agreement,* which provides that despite the statute of limitations, the facts named in, and settled by, the government never will be questioned by either party. But the Service can set aside a closing agreement by showing that it was obtained by fraud or a misrepresentation of a material fact.

4.
What Big Brother Already Knows About You

As a matter of ordinary common sense, one doesn't play cards with people who can read his cards. And if you try to play games with the Internal Revenue Service, that is what is likely to happen. Regardless of how close to your chest you hold your cards, the Service may be able to know what you have. So that you may avoid embarrassing explanations, controversies, or worse (see Chapter 8, "Fines and Penalties"), you should be aware of how complete a file the I.R.S. has accumulated under your name or, more accurately, under your Social Security account number. And if it feels the need, the Service has the apparatus for finding out a great deal more.

The federal taxing authorities automatically receive a tremendous inflow of income data about people. More can be obtained simply by asking for it, the request often being accompanied by a subpoena, summons, or polite suggestion that "cooperation" would be welcomed. Other information is literally thrust at the Internal Revenue Service by people who, for reasons of patriotism, anger, jealousy, or plain greed want the Service to have it.

In order to avoid big trouble, ponder well the words of one Commissioner of Internal Revenue to a Congressional Subcommittee on Appropriations a few years ago: "We have more information about more people than any other agency in this country." Another Commissioner informed a state bar association that "the Internal Revenue Service has powers granted to no other investigative agency to secure the additional information necessary to administer and enforce the tax laws."

Information Returns

All persons engaged in a trade or business and making payments in connection with it to another person of rent, salaries, premiums, annuities, or other fixed or determinable gains, profits, and income of $600 or more in any taxable year must advise the Internal Revenue Service of each payee, his Social Security account number, and the dollar amount by February 28 for the recently closed year. "Fixed" income means a definite, predetermined amount. "Determinable" refers to any situation where there is a basis of calculation by which an amount can be computed, such as a percentage of a company's profits or a proportion of sales revenue which was generated by the payee. These amounts need not be paid annually or at regular intervals.

The minimum amounts which must be reported to the Internal Revenue Service by payors are $10 in the case of dividends and interest. The figure is $1,200 in the case of operators of bingo games or slot machines; it is $1,500 in the case of keno. This refers not only to cash pay-outs but to merchandise or other property worth these amounts. The payor reports retail market values for merchandise, although the recipient has the opportunity to prove, if he can, that the reported values were too high.

Penalties are imposed to ensure that payors submit these records of payment, known as Form 1099. There are many variations on this form, depending upon the nature of the payment. There are 1099–DIV and 1099–INT, which refer, of course, to payments of dividends and of interest, respectively. Form 1099–MED covers payments to physicians or other providers of services under health, accident, and sickness insurance plans or medical association programs. Form 1099L covers payments of $600 or more in a year by a corporation to its shareholders when the company is liquidating. Form 1099–MISC covers such disbursements as payments and awards to persons who are not employees of the payor.

Form 1099 is not required where information is called for by other mechanisms, as these data are available to the Internal Revenue Service already. This includes such situations as shares of a partnership's income of each type, which are reported on the partnership federal income tax return, Form 1065. Amounts paid or payable to beneficiaries are reported to the Service by the fiduciary, such as an executor or a trustee. One form of income tax applies to certain eligible small business companies, known as Subchapter S corporations, where it is the stockholders who are taxed directly and not the corporation; information about this is supplied by the corporation on Form 1120S. By far the most common type of income information supplied to the I.R.S. by payors is Form W–2, which must be used in the case of salary and similar payments. A variation on this is form W–2P, "Statement for Recipients of Annuities, Pensions, or Retired Pay."

The payor is required to give to each payee a copy of the form supplied to the Internal Revenue Service. This has led to some serious traps. The fact that the payor has failed to submit one of these required information forms to the I.R.S. does not mean that the payee is free of tax, for his obligation as taxpayer remains regardless of technical shortcomings by the payor. Where the payee receives a copy of the information form, as he does in most instances, he should use it to check his records and the payor's, for the Service is just about certain to send the payee a query about differences between his federal income tax return and what the payor reported.

People often fall into the trap of believing that because payments in excess of $600, or $10, or whatever is required for different types of income *must* be reported, a payment of a lesser amount, such as $540 rather than $600, will not be made known to the Internal Revenue Service. Actually, many payors report every cent disbursed regardless of amount. This may be because the payor doesn't want to see the payee get away without having his full income taxed. Or it may be simpler to report all payments without having anyone stop to consider even momentarily whether a certain payment should be reported.

Another common trap is complacency about the Internal Revenue Service's inability to match reported payments and the individual income tax returns of recipients. There are countless millions of Forms 1099, W–2, and all the rest which are dumped upon the I.R.S. each year by payors. If a firm in Alaska makes a payment to a person in Florida, how does this fact become known to the Revenue Agent who examines the recipient's income tax return? Until recently, the odds were strong that the payor's piece of paper and the recipient's tax return never got together. But now in most instances they do. The figures on Form 1099 or its relations are fed into an electronic data processing system, such as one of those contraptions at the National Computer Center in West Virginia, known as The Monster of Martinsburg. The key factor is each payee's Social Security account number. Through the modern wizardry of magnetic tape, pay-out data from parties all over the place get on an individual's tax history as assembled by the Internal Revenue Service. When a Revenue Agent asks you how much you received last year from the Tinyville Savings Bank, he already knows. In consequence, your reply will help him to decide the extent to which he can accept the other figures on your tax returns. If you were "careless" in one place, quite likely you were in others also, and nothing can be taken for granted on your return. Even if a patient knew that he did not have to file an information return on Form

1099 for payment for services rendered to Junior by Dr. Scalpel because these payments did not occur in connection with the payor's trade or business, anyone claiming a medical expense deduction is obliged to itemize his payments to physicians. The eager computers pick it up from there. A Revenue Agent assigned to verify a doctor's income tax return has a pretty good idea in advance of what income should appear there, although of course only the larger patient payments ordinarily get listed as back-up data for the medical expense deduction.

The Internal Revenue Service reported in 1977 that in a single year, its automatic data processing equipment found more than four hundred thousand instances of where a payor had reported amounts that the payee "forgot" to report on his own income tax return. More than 70% of these payees admitted their oversights. The Service commented ominously, "The IRS document-matching program is being continued and expanded . . ."

The I.R.S. has stated that for 1980 income tax verification, more than 80% of payors' information reports will be matched to the individual tax returns of the recipients and that this percentage is building up steadily.

Knowing that this stupendous information system hinges upon matching payments and payees through the use of each individual's Social Security account numbers, predictably some persons have tried to beat the system by making use of the account numbers of other persons who are in very low tax brackets or who may not even have enough taxable income to be taxed at all. A payor, before handing over any money, can demand the name and Social Security account number of the actual owner of the right to payment, and the I.R.S. is notified if there are difficulties about getting this information. At places where there are many payments to persons unknown, such as at betting windows of racetracks, the cashier or accountant responsible for supplying information to the Service on Form W–2G (gambling income) insists upon identification in the form of a driver's license, Social Security card, voter registration card, and the like. A new breed of middleman has come into being in this connection: the "five-percenter," who, in return for a certain percentage, will cash winning tickets after supplying his own identification at the cashier's window, all of this, of course, being under the watchful eye of the true (if that's really the word) owner of the winning ticket. In return for his 5%, however, the helpful middleman can be found guilty of aiding in the preparation and presentation of a false tax return. There are penalties for perjury and for conspiracy.

A taxpayer is at a great disadvantage in a controversy with the Internal

Revenue Service, when the super-efficient print-out of a computer produces figures which are different from a taxpayer's rather casual records. Who would dare to argue with the mathematical precision of a computer? But not all courts automatically will give their verdicts to the machines. In one case, a computer announced that more tax was due, without detailed specifics, and the aggrieved taxpayer fought it out in court. He was lucky enough to appear before a judge who was not overawed by electronic data processing. "The computer is a marvelous device that can perform countless tasks at high speed and low cost," declared His Honor, "but it must be used with care. That is because it can also make errors at high speed." What had happened here, the court believed, was the GIGO Rule of Computers (Garbage In, Garbage Out). You can't get reliable figures from a computer unless you first crank in reliable figures, and the Internal Revenue Service was ordered to produce credible information as to the so-called tax deficiency or to drop its claim.

Specialized Forms of Information

Without attempting to compile a complete catalog, there are presented here some of the other forms of information which is made available to the Internal Revenue Service.

Employees are required to report to their employers the amount of tips received in a calendar month if they amount to $20 or more. Records of tips are supposed to be kept by employees on Form 4070A. The employer includes this amount on the regular Form W–2 he submits for each employee where required.

In a 1979 case, the Internal Revenue Service was permitted to reconstruct the income of an individual where his records were sketchy. The source of the damning information was a computer print-out prepared by the Bureau of Data Processing, Social Security Administration.

Contractors must report payments of $600 or more in a year to subcontractors under certain circumstances.

Blue Cross–Blue Shield is called upon to submit reports of payments of $600 or more to physicians.

Banks are required to report to the government monthly transactions involving (1) $2,500 or more of United States currency in denominations of $100 or higher, (2) $10,000 or more in U.S. currency in any denomination, and (3) transactions in any amount in any denomination which management deems to be "unusual." In general, this does not apply in the case of transfers between bankers, nor in the case of transactions between a bank and an established customer involving amounts which the bank reasonably may conclude are not excessive in terms of the usual conduct of the customer's business.

Banks must report shipments of cash or various financial documents "as good as cash" where $5,000 or more is involved, if the money goes from the United States to a place outside of the country, or vice versa.

Many financial institutions offer merchandise to persons who induce other people to make time deposits. The value of the merchandise depends upon the size of the induced deposit. Fair market value of this merchandise is includible in the recipient's gross income. To make certain that he remembers to report this non-cash item, the I.R.S. in 1980 ordered financial institutions to file an information return where the fair market value of a gift is $600 or more.

Some information which must be supplied to the Internal Revenue Service is highly particularized. For example, fishing boat operators must supply information about the percentage of a catch which is allocated to the individuals participating in a venture.

A self-employed person may fail to file federal income tax returns in the belief that inasmuch as he has no employer to report his salary payments, the I.R.S won't know of his earnings. But this same person, especially as he approaches retirement age, will be interested in getting his Federal Insurance Contributions Act ("Social Security") pension. So he is apt to report self-employment income to the Social Security Administration. Perhaps some federal agencies aren't on speaking terms with other federal agencies. But as a 1980 case shows, the I.R.S. and the S.S.A. do check with each other on such matters.

Summonses

For the purpose of finding out the correctness of a person's federal income tax return or the determination of proper tax liability, the Internal Revenue Service is authorized by law to examine any books, papers, records, or other data which may be of use. The I.R.S. may issue summonses for the disclosure of any information not only to a taxpayer or to any of his employees, but also to *any* party having possession or care of books of account containing entries relating to a taxpayer's income. This can include banks, brokerage firms, accountants, or anyone else not protected by *privilege,* a subject which will be discussed in Chapter 9.

Typically, the Service may summon a bank to produce photocopies of bank statements, cancelled checks, and deposit slips on all accounts on which named parties could write checks or make withdrawals, including savings accounts. Also, a bank may be required to supply photocopies of all financial statements of specified taxpayers on file with the bank, as in connection with bank loan applications. Photocopies may be requisitioned in the case of all loans and related interest, and likewise copies of any trust agreements in which the bank was a trustee. The third party covered by a summons may have to produce any records kept in the ordinary course of business.

If a taxpayer is a depositor or customer in a foreign bank which is under the control of a bank within the jurisdiction of the Internal Revenue Service, the controlling bank can be served with a summons to have the branch bank's records made available, even if the records are in a foreign country. Such was the situation where a New York bank had to produce records of an independent branch in the Republic of Panama.

The Internal Revenue Service may issue a "John Doe" summons to banks to obtain information about unidentified persons who have had transactions which suggest the possibility of unpaid taxes. The United States Supreme Court approved this technique when a Federal Reserve bank tipped off the Service that someone had been depositing numerous large-denomination bills of ancient vintage in a certain bank. It was held that the I.R.S. had the right to see the bank's records in order to identify the mysterious depositor. Doubtless he received an official visitor shortly thereafter.

A financial institution may wish to be known as a friendly bank, not only to customers but to the Internal Revenue Service. Helping the latter may antagonize the former. So when a bank is asked by Revenue Agents to turn over customer records, the bank may ask for a "courtesy summons" as a protection. Then the irate customer can be told, "We had no choice. Here's the summons which was served upon us."

The Internal Revenue Service may check up on the number of dependents to which an individual is entitled on his federal income tax return by visiting his employer. Form W–4, the withholding exemption certificate filed by each employee with his employer, provides this information. Additionally, an employer is likely to have information about dependents of an employee for personnel records purposes. Employers may very well cooperate with the I.R.S. in any inquiries about employees, even when there is no legal compulsion, because of an understandable desire not to incur the displeasure of the Service, which can be expressed in so many ways.

Your Own Accountant May Have to Lead I.R.S. to Items You Fear Will Be Disallowed

It is customary for many accounting firms to prepare workpapers in order to evaluate the sufficiency of a business client's reserves to meet its possible tax liabilities. These workpapers are based in part upon the accountant's evaluation of opinions and guesses communicated in confidence by the client. The accountant considers all uncertain tax positions taken by the client, who customarily resolves all legitimate doubts in his own favor, and determines whether the reserves are sufficient to cover any additional tax liability that could result if questionable items were decided against the client by the I.R.S. The Service can compel an accountant to turn over such analyses during the audit of a taxpayer's return, for there is no accountant-client privilege of confidentiality. That means, in the words of a 1980 decision, that the accountant upon the Service's demand must reveal "soft spots where IRS could profitably probe."

I.R.S. May Be Monitoring Your Mail

The Internal Revenue Service is permitted to obtain information about a taxpayer's affairs, by summons if necessary, from anyone who has facts and figures that could relate to the taxpayer's income, provided no criminal prosecution has been recommended as yet to the Department of Justice. In order to learn who might have interesting information about one taxpayer, the I.R.S. got the U.S. Postal Service to monitor his mail. This involved only identification of senders or recipients of correspondence with the taxpayer and not the opening of mail. But it could lead the tax people to persons who could be induced, one way or another, to tell what they know. A 1980 case involved one taxpayer who asked a court to intervene as this stealthy method of investigation amounted to harassment. The court refused.

The Right to Privacy

The Privacy Act of 1975 requires that the Internal Revenue Service or other federal agency requesting information from individuals:

1. Cite the authority which authorizes the solicitation of the information.

2.   State whether the submission of the required information is voluntary or mandatory.

3.   Explain the principal use of the required information.

4.   State the routine uses which also may be made of the information.

5.   Indicate the effects on the individual who does not provide the requested information ("or else").

Other Governmental Agencies

Various governmental enforcement agencies, such as the Department of Justice, automatically inform the Internal Revenue Service of anything learned about an individual which may have federal income tax consequences, such as the existence of bribes or extortion money which presumably was not reported on an income tax return.

By a form of treaty, the Internal Revenue Service and each of the states has an arrangement calling for an exchange of information about what either party has unearthed about a taxpayer. A state tax auditor, because of his contacts or familiarity with local conditions, might learn something about an individual's tax irregularities, which facts are transmitted to the I.R.S. "for appropriate action."

Unauthorized Disclosures by I.R.S.

It is apparent from the earlier portions of this chapter that a tremendous amount of personal and confidential data is fed to and stored by the Internal Revenue Service. In an effort to prevent invasion of privacy beyond what is deemed to be necessary for tax purposes, the Tax Reform Act of 1976 provided that any taxpayer damaged by unlawful disclosure of information by a governmental employee can bring suit against him, provided there was a willful or negligent disclosure of information which, by law, was confidential. A court cannot make an award of less than $1,000 for each instance of unauthorized disclosure. In addition to recompense for actual damage these leaks have caused you, punitive damages also are authorized when the unlawful disclosure was deliberate or the result of gross negligence. The malicious or careless governmental employee will be reimbursed by the government only if the disclosure took place in the performance of his official duties relating to tax administration.

The Tax Informant

Impressive as is the size and efficiency of the Internal Revenue Service automatic data processing system, it is reassuring to learn that the machine has not superseded people in one area at least. According to a statement made to newspaper publishers by the Director of the Federal Bureau of Investigation in 1978, Americans must accept the fact that informers are "the most effective tool in law enforcement today." Law enforcement, of course, includes the enforcement of tax law.

An important and usually unsuspected reason for a person's income tax return to be selected by the I.R.S. for examination is a direct tipoff by someone in position to know what is going on. Obviously, the Internal Revenue Service cannot possibly check every income tax return, or devote to each one the time and care necessary to ferret out any improprieties. And many instances of income concealment, expense padding, and distortion of facts and figures are so cunningly hidden that unless a Revenue Agent is given a good clue, the matter is likely to go undetected. But there are many people who are determined that you shall not get away with it.

Persons may have any one of many reasons for telling the Internal Revenue Service of somebody else's tax cheating, real or imaginary. Personal hatred, envy of another party's success, the desire to be a good citizen, the opportunity to release one's pent-up displeasure at being snubbed or discharged, hope of being promotoed to the post which had been held by a disgraced superior, and greed are all important reasons which lead to an individual to tell all.

If a taxpayer (or non-taxpayer) is dishonest about his income and expenses, of course there is additional tax for the Internal Revenue Service to assess, along with interest and penalty. A person who is familiar with the situation can guide the Service to trouble spots. But there are numerous instances where a person's tax can be increased greatly even if he has been completely honest. In perfectly good faith, he may have omitted to report all of his income correctly through sheer ignorance or carelessness. Obviously, the tax law can be very complicated, and the requirements often are difficult to meet even if one is trying to do everything which is required of him. There may be items which are perfectly proper deductions, except that the taxpayer is unable to substantiate them, such as contributions, medical expenditures, casualty losses, business entertainment, and the like, where receipts, vouchers, and other documents have been lost or destroyed. If a Revenue Agent is led to zero in on unsupported business travel, for example, there will be an automatic tax disallowance, even though the taxpayer could not in any sense be said to be dishonest or a cheat. Any mistake or oversight made by a taxpayer could lead to additional income tax, should the matter be brought to the attention of the Internal Revenue Service.

In one year, the Internal Revenue Service reported, it received 160,000 leads to investigate. These could range from overlooked income, mislabeled transactions, bribes to police officials for overlooking traffic or more serious violations of law, income or deductions which had been reported in an incorrect year, and capital gains or losses computed incorrectly, to elaborate schemes of fictitious accounts or buried income.

An informer could be *anyone:* an employee (especially one who was discharged or passed over for promotion), a social acquaintance who overheard something at a dinner party, a jealous brother-in-law who had opportunity to snoop around in one's desk, an accountant who felt he was shortchanged on his fee, a busybody telephone operator . . . the list is virtually endless. In the case of a business, the one who blows the whistle is frequently someone in a very responsible position, for he is the one most likely to know the company's secrets and weaknesses: the chief accountant, the office manager, a vice-president who was retired for age. In one case, it was a corporation's controller who informed the I.R.S. that the company's entire executive travel and entertainment deduction could be disallowed because the company had no documents to support these deductions. How was he so certain that the corporation could not justify its deductions? Because, as soon as he was given notice of dismissal, he himself had removed these indispensable records from the company files.

Ordinarily, any "finding" made by the I.R.S. is presumed to be correct, and it is up to the taxpayer to refute it if he can. This applies to anything furnished by a respectable third-party citizen informant. But a 1979 decision refused to require a taxpayer to disprove charges made by a former employee who wanted to gain favor with the authorities so that they would treat him generously in a criminal matter in which he was involved. Informants frequently act out of reasons of revenge and jealousy, which motives do not make their revelation any less valuable. But this person's character and personal motives undermined his believability as a witness, and an I.R.S. finding based upon what he said did not have to be refuted by the taxpayer.

There are two types of tax leaks that supply information to the Internal Revenue Service. First, there is the so-called squeal letter, which is written, sometimes anonymously, to the Service about alleged tax crimes or weaknesses of someone else. As a whole, these letters are not too helpful to the I.R.S., for they are apt to be written because of anger or spite by someone who does not really have knowledge of all the facts and who is not technically competent to gather enough specifics to enable the Service to make an assessment. "Squeal letters" may come from envious neighbors who cannot afford to buy a swimming pool as you have done, or a rejected fiancée, or from a typist who overheard part of a secret conversation. Writers of these letters usually are amateurs without full comprehension of all that is involved.

The second class of person who clues in the I.R.S. to what may be found involves a far more serious situation. This is the professional tax informant, who generally is in position to know something and who is willing to spend the necessary time to develop the facts which the Service must have in order to act. The tax informant may be a responsible business associate, a trusted friend, a professional advisor who understands the tax law, the substantiation requirements, and the taxpayer's own records and accounts. He is in position to cash in on his professionalism very handsomely, and he knows it. If a would-be informant goes to the I.R.S. before he presents his facts, he can make a deal with the Service, which is authorized to enter into a written agreement with him to pay him up to 10% of any additional federal tax recovered as a result of his leads, if it appears that without his help, the government would not have been able to collect these moneys. This agreement is made on Form 211. Without such an agreement prior to his revelation, his reward will be whatever the I.R.S. chooses to give him, a matter in which no court will interfere regardless of how inadequate the reward may seem. In one case an informant, without any written agreement, gave the Service evidence with which to collect more than $1,000,000 in taxes which otherwise would not have been collected. He was paid an insulting $17,000. Is that any way to try to attract business?

As a matter of fact, the Internal Revenue Service seems to be embarrassed at the whole idea of paying for personal help in this day of sophisticated data processing equipment and a large staff of highly trained, intelligent Revenue Agents. And peaching on someone else is not well regarded by most people. "The Revenue Service," said a spokesperson, "is fully aware of the distasteful implications to Americans of any actions which involve the spying of one individual on another, and its policy in administering the law is geared to avoid specific encouragement of such action." Accordingly, "It is Revenue Service policy that there shall be no general appeals to members of the public to inform on other individuals. . . . But," continues the statement, "the Internal Revenue Service would be remiss in its duties if it refused to consider allegations of evasion solely on the ground that the source was distasteful. The plain fact is that the Revenue Service does recover substantial amounts of taxes and penalties as a result of information furnished by informants."

In return for his information, the tax informant can receive not only money but something which may prove to be even more valuable: the keeping secret of his identity. The United States Constitution provides the right to confront one's accuser in a criminal action, which includes tax evasion. But the Supreme Court has said that this does not apply in the case of an informant whose revelations might not be made if they placed him in personal jeopardy. This makes it possible and safe for a taxpayer's brother, his secretary, his assistant, his banker, or anyone else to report to the I.R.S. Decided cases have revealed that informants have been killed in the line of performance of what they regarded as their duty or conduct of their business. To prevent this sort of thing, the Freedom of Information Act provides that information in the possession of governmental agencies must, with certain exceptions, be revealed to persons affected, but the identity of the party who furnished this information is confidential.

It was held in a 1980 decision that a person who provides tax leads to the I.R.S. without compensation (a "squeal letter") also is entitled to have his identity kept confidential if the unmasked taxpayer wants to know who blew the whistle. As President Carter said when signing legislation to protect an informant's identity even where he is an unpaid amateur. "A citizen must be able to complain to his Government and to provide information."

Under the Freedom of Information Act, a person can require the I.R.S. to produce documents relating to his Federal income tax return. Exception: investigatory records compiled for law enforcement purposes, production of which would disclose the identity of a confidential source. A taxpayer was not entitled to learn the name of a person who had made a telephone call to a person assigned to "Informants Duty" at an Internal Revenue Service office in Baltimore, declared a 1980 decision.

There are certain steps a taxpayer can take to minimize the risks presented by a tax informant. He should be very careful about who is present when he discusses financial and tax matters. His desk and file cabinets should be locked at all times when he is not present. He should be careful about boasting how much smarter he is than the revenuers, as, for example, when he . . . If he discharges an office or household employee, it would be better to pay off this person at once in lieu of notice, before there is opportunity for the aggrieved party to copy or to filch papers and other records. He should make every effort to see that an employee, associate, or consultant does not go away mad.

Your spouse can turn you in. It is widely believed that one's spouse cannot testify against you in a criminal matter, such as tax evasion. Such is not the case. Formerly, one's spouse could not be *compelled* to testify against you, but in 1980, the United States Supreme Court reversed its own decision of twenty-two years previously that one spouse can't be compelled to testify against the other in a federal court. In any case, one spouse can always testify against another in a tax matter if she (some pronoun has to be used here, and this one was selected at random) chooses to do so. What she says may have modest tax impact, as where one woman stated that her husband had a schnauzer dog named Max Donovan on his payroll. Or she may have a great deal to reveal. So one should be as careful about speaking of his tax cleverness in front of his spouse as in front of anyone else. And he should be just as careful about keeping locks locked.

5.
The Advantages
of Being a Pack Rat

It has been mentioned previously that in virtually every situation which you are likely to encounter, the burden of proof is upon the taxpayer. Proof rarely can be established retroactively. This means that substantiation, verification, documentation must be contemporary with what you are trying to prove. To convince the Internal Revenue Service that something happened or didn't happen when you claim, customarily this requires the maintenance of pieces of paper: bills, letters, ticket stubs, photographs, accounting entries, cancelled checks, receipts, and the like. The saving of income taxes can depend upon the pooled intelligence of long-experienced lawyers, accountants, and other specialists. It can depend equally upon a very simple matter of good housekeeping: retention of various pieces of paper so that they can be produced when necessary—that is, when you have that encounter session with a Revenue Agent. In the language of the computer age, you must have a good retrieval system.

Keeping Required Records Isn't Regarded as
Enforced Slavery

The keeping of records in order to substantiate Internal Revenue Service rules for documenting deductions is so time-consuming, claimed one businessperson, that it places a taxpayer in a position of involuntary servitude. And that is forbidden by the Thirteenth Amendment to the United States Constitution. Perhaps it amounted to servitude, it was held in a 1979 decision, but it wasn't involuntary. A person isn't forced to claim a tax deduction. If he does not claim it, he won't be bothered by I.R.S. rules as to substantiating it.

What to Keep

A person must keep records, substantiation, and explanations for everything which appears on his federal income tax return, or which the Internal Revenue Service thinks should appear there. This covers every conceivable type of item, from charitable contributions to proof that you are married. There is nothing too small for the I.R.S. to question—and to disallow. If a disallowance is worth saving, if nontaxable receipts are important enough so that it is worth your while to keep them untaxed, substantiation must be available to support your point of view.

In addition, claimed deductions which you cannot substantiate, in the words of one court decision, "create doubt as to the accuracy of the total deduction." Where an item on the tax return cannot be supported, a negligence penalty may be imposed because reasonable care had not been taken to reflect income and deductions.

How Long Must Back-Up Material Be Kept?

Records must be kept for as long as federal income tax returns are "open" for tax audit. In most instances, the statute of limitations will close a tax return three years from the date the return was due or filed, or two years from the date the tax was paid, whichever occurs later. If gross income has been understated by more than 25%, the three-year period is extended to six years; and this easily can come about because of an honest misunderstanding as to the year in which certain income should have been reported. The statute of limitations may be extended for an agreed period, as where the parties agree to await a court decision in somebody else's tax dispute of a similar nature, or where the taxpayer or the Revenue Agent is seriously ill. There is no statute of limitations in the case of fraud, which means that a tax return and its supporting material always are open for examination.

When a corporation has been dissolved, its unpaid federal income taxes may be collected from any shareholder up to the value of the property he has received in the liquidation. The I.R.S. can collect this up to one year after the corporation's statute of limitations has expired, even if a shareholder's own limitation period otherwise would have expired.

Where a person's tax return does not contain enough information so that tax computation properly can be made and verified, this is regarded as "no return." The statute of limitations never begins if no return in a meaningful sense has been filed. So the time for audit never ends. That means it always is open season for I.R.S. hunters.

An individual has the opportunity of "averaging" his income, such as when his income in a particular year is substantially larger than it had been in the four previous taxable years. In that event, records must be kept for each of these previous years. Averaging can produce worthwhile tax savings.

In certain instances, records must be kept as long as a person holds property covered by these records. For example, if he sells securities or his home, gain or loss on that transaction is based upon the difference between what he paid for the property and what he receives for it, frequently with adjustments for certain transactions during this period. To establish his gain or loss, he must be able to prove what he paid for the property, which may have been twenty or more years ago. Cost figures also may have to be proven in the case of a casualty loss, regardless of how long ago the property was acquired. As will be mentioned later in this chapter, it may be necessary to prove what somebody else paid for property, perhaps as far back as 1913. This is the situation where a person sells property which he had received by gift.

Legislation sometimes is enacted which provides relief for taxpayers if they can establish facts that can be proven only by records of transactions in prior years. If you destroy records which could have thrown light on the proper treatment of some item on your federal income tax return, the courts will presume that you destroyed this material so that it could not reveal facts or figures which were against your interest. Then the courts are apt to take the position that you permitted the destruction of the records in order to avoid the tax consequences of what they would have revealed.

Where to Keep Records

According to the Treasury Department regulations, all required records must be kept "at one or more convenient and safe locations accessible to internal revenue officers . . ." Note that word "safe."

If necessary records, such as the cost of your home, securities, jewelry, and the like are kept in a desk drawer at home, they could be lost should there be a fire. All too frequently, papers which could have established the tax loss where a building was burned were destroyed at the same time that the building was. The bill for a valuable piece of jewelry might be kept in the leather box containing the jewelry, and both could be stolen at the same time.

Important back-up materials for a tax return might be kept in a safe deposit box at your bank, or in your accountant's office. Where the amounts involved are large enough to justify the expense, supporting evidence could be microfilmed or photocopied for safe storage at some other location.

Where "Proof" Is Not Accepted as Proof

For federal income tax purposes, payment by check rather than cash furnishes a far more acceptable form of proof. Now there is a paper trail, something to show to a Revenue Agent. In addition, old checkbooks and canceled checks are far more likely to be found in one place than are loose receipts for cash should a tax examiner ask questions. Bills, receipts, and memoranda may be difficult to round up.

But even if an explanation of a payment appears on a person's checkbook stub, that does not necessarily supply proof of entitlement to a tax deduction. A thorough Revenue Agent may dig around sufficiently to relate the checkbook stub to an invoice or other record of what the payment actually represented. In one case, the checkbook notation for a businessperson's payment read "Dies and jigs for job #121214." What the invoice showed for the payment was two diamond rings. "Factory maintenance" was the explanation given for the purchase of a piano, which apparently had not been shipped to the employees' cafeteria. "Factory supplies" was noted in the checkbook for an invoice which was for a six-piece sterling silver tea set. Payment for a silver fox scarf was described as "General expense." The cost of a mink jacket was identified on the checkbook stub as "Maintenance," without reference to whose. This taxpayer's reliance upon his checkbook rather than actual bills in preparing his tax return resulted in his conviction for fraud.

One businessman who unquestionably travelled away from home in connection with his commercial activities attempted to substantiate his travel expenses with cancelled checks payable to hotels in the various cities he had to visit. But the actual bill of one of these hotels showed that disbursements charged to his account included a bill for feminine wearing apparel.

Another area in which checks are not proof of an income tax deduction is charitable deductions. In support of his tax return deduction, an individual may show the Revenue Agent a check to a tax-exempt university, properly endorsed and negotiated. But in the absence of further documentation, the check may be disregarded as inconclusive. The taxpayer may merely have been paying his son's non-deductible tuition or dormitory charges, the check being for an even amount such as contributions normally would be, the balance being paid in cash. Or the payment to the university may have been for a pair of season tickets for football games.

Even receipts do not prove one's right to a tax deduction. A receipt, or a funds solicitation letter, may state that "Contributions are tax deductible," which means nothing if the organization is not, or no longer is, on the Treasury Department's list of organizations, contributions to which are deductible. An approved charitable organization, such as a church, may sell tickets to a play, or chances in a raffle, the tickets or the accompanying literature being marked "Tax-deductible." But the fact that the charitable organization thus characterized the "contribution" does not make it so for tax purposes. In the case of the theatre tickets, all that is deductible is the excess of the cost over the box office price. If a person gets anything in return for his "donation," it is not a contribution but an exchange for value. Even in the case of a church-sponsored drawing for a car, the "contributor" is getting something in return. Here, it may be a one-in-a-hundred-thousand chance of winning the car.

Merchandisers of credit cards often stress in their advertisements that use of such cards assures a tax deduction for business entertaining and travel. One major New York City bank stated in its ads: "Like other cards it gives you a clear record of your expenditures, gives you proof of travel, entertainment and hotel bills for the Internal Revenue Service . . ." Certainly this is misleading advertising, for as will be mentioned later in this chapter, the I.R.S. requires more than that before deduction is allowed.

Business diaries similarly are frequently advertised, usually in December or January, as being assurance that all possible tax deductions will be allowed. That certainly is not the case, for reference to the fact that on September 4 you lunched at the Café Splendide with John Dough is not proof that this was a business meeting. For example, it is required that the taxpayer show the business purpose for this meal. What business was discussed? What other persons were present? The Internal Revenue Service will accept diary entries as substantiation for business meals up to $25. That does not cover an appropriately impressive business meal these days.

A cancelled check payable to an attorney is not indication of tax deductibility. Was the payment for business purposes (usually deductible) or for personal purposes (customarily non-deductible)? For example, the payment might have covered a lawyer's fee for negotiating a twenty-year lease for a business tenant. The tenant can deduct only one-twentieth of this fee each year for the next twenty years. The payment might have been for a non-deductible purpose, such as where the lawyer handled an alimony settlement or arranged to have a traffic ticket for drunken driving "fixed."

The point is that cancelled checks in themselves prove nothing as to tax deductibility. The taxpayer must also have available some evidence of what the payments actually represented: for example, a receipt from a university's building fund committee or a lawyer's bill which specifies the nature of the actual services rendered.

Keep Your Old Tax Returns

It was mentioned earlier in this chapter that the statute of limitations bars the reopening of a federal income tax return after a certain number of years, depending upon the circumstances. But tax returns can be very useful even if the statute of limitations has expired.

For example, a taxpayer has claimed a deduction in the taxable year. Actually the deduction should have been taken in an earlier year. So the Internal Revenue Service may allege fraud, that is, taking the same deduction in two different years. If you have kept a copy of your return for the earlier year, this may show that the deduction was not taken at that time.

Some transactions straddle a period of several years, such as in the case of installment sales or advance payments. You or your new accountant may want to see how an ongoing transaction had been reported on the tax returns of earlier years.

Certain losses or deductions which cannot be fully utilized in one taxable year may be carried over into other years. A net operating loss may not be utilized in a particular year because there is insufficient income to absorb it. The loss may be carried back for three years, starting with the earliest, and then carried forward for seven years to the extent that it has not been used up, starting with the first succeeding year. To apply the carryback correctly, it is necessary to have the tax returns for those years. In the case of capital losses, an individual has an unlimited loss carryforward; but his computations will require retention of the tax returns for years in which the losses occurred. An individual may make charitable contributions in excess of the allowable deduction for that year, which is a percentage of his adjusted gross income, the percentage depending upon the nature of the contribution. There is a five-year carryover of unused contributions. Here, again, reference to previous tax returns is necessary to see the extent to which the carryover has been utilized.

If you have not kept, or cannot find, your federal income tax returns of previous years, you can obtain copies from the Internal Revenue Service by filing Form 4506, "Request For Copy Of Tax Return." In general, the Service keeps copies of tax returns for seven years.

The custodian of records at the Internal Revenue Service Center where a tax return has been filed will furnish a transcript at the price of $1 a page. Tax returns are kept at the service center where filed for at least six months. Then they are transferred to a Federal Records Center, where they remain for seven years. Eventually the returns are transferred back to the original service center, where they remain forever.

Keep Records Showing What Isn't Income

Data should be kept to identify everything that comes in, whether in the form of cash or the equivalent. All receipts are deemed by the Internal Revenue Service to represent taxable income, unless you can prove to the contrary. So it is necessary to be able to identify all input items, such as loan repayments, borrowing, gifts, inheritances, refunds of cash deposits or insurance company premiums, and tranfers from other accounts.

An individual might receive a cash settlement from his employer or from somebody else which may or may not represent taxable income. It is up to him to keep record of what the payment really represents, or it will be taxed as income. For example, suppose an employee was discharged for dishonesty by the company for which he works as sales manager. He files suit against the company for breach of contract. Meanwhile, the ex-employee suffers a nervous breakdown as the result of what he feels is permanent disgrace: how will he be able to face his old friends, how will he be able to find another job in view of this smear on his record, etc.? To settle the controversy, the company agrees to pay him a certain sum of money, and the lawsuit is dropped. If the amount he receives is regarded as dismissal pay, it is fully taxable as ordinary income. If the amount represents payment for wrongful discharge, restitution for personal damage sustained (disgrace or the breakdown), or the righting of a wrong, the amount is not taxable income. In general, all moneys flowing from employer to employee or even ex-employee are deemed by the I.R.S. to be a form of compensation, for why else would they be paid? The employee should keep available a record of what the payment actually represents. If it is damages for injuries sustained, have the employer say so in writing. Or keep a file of correspondence which proves the matter.

An individual may be the beneficiary of a scholarship from his employer, either receiving the money himself or having it paid directly to an educational institution by his employer. Ordinarily, any economic benefit which an employee receives by reason of the employer-employee relationship is regarded as taxable income. But a student can exclude from his gross income the value of a scholarship or fellowship grant at an educational institution where he is a candidate for a degree. He must keep data which prove that his course of study (except in one limited area) is not for the benefit of the employer; that the amounts received are not compensation for past, present, or future services; and that he is not required to work for the provider of this scholarship after his education is completed. Exclusion of scholarship is permitted to a limited extent in the case of persons who are not candidates for a degree.

If an employer voluntarily makes payments to the spouse of an employee who dies in service while on the payroll, the tax treatment of this payment to the widow(er) depends upon what this amount had been intended to be. Where as so often is the case, the payment was made in recognition of the deceased employee's valuable services, it is fully taxable. The surviving spouse should preserve any correspondence with the employer to establish, if possible, that the payment actually was a tax-free gift. For example, was the survivor asked any questions about financial needs and resources after the employee's untimely death? Such a question would indicate that the payment had been intended as a gift prompted by economic distress.

Interest on state and municipal bonds is tax-free and should be so noted in one's income records; a mere notation such as ''bond interest'' would bring about unnecessary taxation. Keep the payor's covering letter or voucher if this was a registered bond and you received a check in the mail. Although corporate dividends generally are fully taxable, distributions in partial liquidation of a corporation are not; the corporation's letter transmitting its check should be retained so that non-taxable income or capital gain can be identified. Distributions received from regulated investment companies (mutual funds) and real estate investment trusts also may be of capital gains as well as ordinary income, and the explanatory letters from the companies themselves should be preserved as part of your tax records.

If a person is a shareholder in a corporation which participates in a tax-free reorganization, the status of stocks, bonds, or cash which he receives can involve tricky tax questions. Ordinarily, a corporation will send a letter to shareholders, advising them that "in the opinion of counsel," such-and-such are the tax consequences. Keep these letters as part of your tax records. They should be preserved for as long as you hold the securities, plus the length of time for the statute of limitations to close the tax years when you sold these securities.

Keep any correspondence you receive from companies whose securities you hold, or brokers who may be retaining such securities for you. Valuable information may be contained here as to the tax status of stock dividends, split-ups, and exchanges.

Ordinarily, any economic benefit which an employee receives from his employer is taxed as compensation. But an employee is not taxed upon the value of housing which he is furnished upon the employer's premises if (1) the employee is required to live there as a condition of his employment and (2) his being there serves a business purpose of the employer. Example: a company's research director is provided with a home close to the plant on company-owned land, so that he will be readily available at any time when an experiment or process requires his attention at unpredictable times. The correspondence setting up and describing the arrangement should be retained so that the non-income character of the arrangement can be made clear to a Revenue Agent.

Interest Payments

Most forms of interest are deductible for tax purposes, whether business or personal indebtedness is involved. But payments to creditors may not entirely represent interest. Monthly payments to a bank or to a building and loan association customarily are part reduction of the mortgage and part interest. Only the latter is deductible. Keep the bank's repayment schedule or other breakdown available in order to prove to the Revenue Agent what part of the payment represents deductible interest.

Department stores, service stations, and other providers of consumer credit charge interest on unpaid balances. Keep a record of these for interest deduction purposes, for most items on bills from these companies are not tax-deductible. Credit card charges often include interest. Keep a record of these. All too often, the only interest a taxpayer deducts is what he pays to a bank. Don't overlook what you have paid to other parties, such as stores—or to even the Internal Revenue Service on a tax bill for a prior period.

71

Medical Expenses

The medical expense deduction is the amount by which such expenses exceed 3% of a person's adjusted gross income for the year. It is necessary to keep bills representing payments to physicians, dentists, hospitals, nurses, etc. Without a cancelled check or a receipted bill, you have no proof that the party listed on your medical expense deduction ever was paid, or that the payment was for you or for a dependent.

Just because a physician recommended that you do or take something doesn't make it a deductible medical expense. To be entitled to the deduction, you must be in position to answer these questions, which were asked by one court: "Was it incurred at the direction or suggestion of a physician; did the treatment bear directly or indirectly on the physical [or mental] condition in question; did the treatment bear such a direct or proximate therapeutic relation to the body condition as to justify a reasonable belief the same would be efficacious; was the treatment so proximate in time to the onset or recurrence of the disease or condition as to make one the true occasion of the other, thus eliminating expense incurred for general, as contrasted with some specific, physical improvements?" "The doctor ordered it" may be sufficient reason for you to spend money, but the Revenue Agent didn't hear what the physician said. Have the doctor put it in writing.

Certain outlays for medical purposes are not deductible because they are characterized as capital expenditures, that is, benefits are obtained which will last for more than one year. For example, a swimming pool or elevator may be placed in a person's home at the direction of a physician for the purpose of improving or maintaining his patient's health. Inasmuch as the assets acquired will last for some years, the cost must be deducted for tax purposes ratably over the entire life of the asset. But to the extent that the cost of the pool, elevator, etc., does not add to the value of the home, this may be deducted currently as medical expenses. The statement of a real estate expert is used to indicate the extent to which the $15,000 cost of the pool actually adds to the value of the home. Keep this statement with your tax records.

In the case of a medical expense, an individual may also be called upon to prove that he was not covered by medical insurance, either directly or through an employer's plan, and that he could not have recovered the cost of any of the medical expenses from anyone even if he had attempted to do so.

Casualty Losses

Casualty losses are fully deductible in the case of assets used for business purposes. Non-business casualty losses are deductible to the extent that they exceed $100. There are several problems of proof here: (1) Was the loss a result of what the tax law defines as a casualty? (2) Was the taxpayer really the one who sustained the economic loss resulting from the casualty? (3) What is the amount of the deductible loss? (4) Was any recovery possible through insurance or otherwise? (5) In what year is the loss deductible for tax purposes?

A casualty for tax purposes is the complete or partial destruction or loss of property resulting from an identifiable event which is damaging to property and which is sudden, unexpected, or unusual in nature. If property is destroyed or damaged, the taxpayer must prove that what happened to it was the result of this definition of a casualty. So you must develop proof of what actually happened.

Loss by theft or embezzlement also qualifies as a casualty for tax purposes. Here the problem of proof can be difficult. The fact that something is missing does not mean that it was stolen. For example, an individual stayed overnight at a motel. Before retiring that night, he placed his diamond ring on a night table next to his bed. He had a cold, and he also placed on this table a supply of facial tissues. The next morning, he threw the used facial tissues into a wastebasket, which was emptied by the cleaning person. Later he realized that his diamond ring was missing. Had it been stolen, as he claimed? Or had he carelessly swept it up with the facial tissues which he dumped into the wastebasket? Inasmuch as he could not prove what actually had happened to the ring, he could not claim a theft loss. Many things *could* have happened to the ring. He might have lent it to a friend. He might have forfeited his right to claim a casualty loss deduction because he had done something grossly negligent, such as leaving the ring directly under a lighted lamp on the ground floor of the motel, where his bedroom window had been wide open.

In order to establish a theft loss, report it to the police at once. Retain proof that you have done so, such as by notation of the policeperson's shield number. If another person is discovered to have your property, you must prosecute, or it can be presumed that you had given away the property or had allowed someone else to use it.

The amount of the casualty loss deduction generally is the lesser of (1) the decrease in the fair market value of the property as the result of the casualty and (2) the adjusted basis of the property. The adjusted basis is cost plus any improvements which improved the value or usefulness of the property less (in the case of business property) depreciation which had been taken or should have been taken. Cost or other basis of the property may be difficult to prove. A business usually has records of what each piece of property costs; an individual rarely has such information in the case of non-business property. One never knows whether or when he will be called upon to prove the amount of a casualty loss. So he should keep all bills and invoices permanently against the possible day of reckoning. If several properties, such as a car and a tractor, were acquired at one time for a single price, the amount paid must be broken down at the time of purchase to show what was paid for *each* asset. Otherwise, should one of the properties be lost through casualty, the Internal Revenue Service may say that the amount of loss was minimal, for the price paid actually represented for the most part the cost of the asset which wasn't destroyed. The taxpayer has the burden of establishing what part of the cost was allocated to *each* property acquired.

Failure to prove the cost or adjusted basis of an asset can mean loss of the casualty deduction. In the absence of proof by the taxpayer, the Internal Revenue Service frequently assigns the figure of zero. Then the lower of cost or fair market value, that is, the amount of the deduction, is zero.

The problem of basis where property was acquired by gift or inheritance will be mentioned later in this chapter.

The actual cost of repairing damaged property to restore it to its original condition may be accepted as the amount of deductible casualty loss. But the taxpayer must prove what the original condition of the property was, that the repairs did no more than restore the property to that condition, and that the repair costs were not excessive.

Proof of the amount of a casualty loss could be very difficult. In one case, after a fire had destroyed a home and its contents, the taxpayer had the testimony of the interior decorator who had furnished the house and who was so familiar with it from his many visits as a consultant and a friend that he could even describe the principal articles of clothing which had been there. In one case involving destruction of a home, an occupant was able to reconstruct from memory an inventory of nineteen hundred items which had been there, with credible estimates of how much each had cost. Admittedly, this proof was exceptional in nature. More commonly used are photographs. Unfortunately, few people think of photographing their homes and contents before a casualty. Think of it right now. The taxpayer would do well to keep a frequently updated inventory of his furniture, ornaments, books, jewelry, musical instruments, and the like. Warning: do not keep the only copy of this inventory at home.

Education

There is no such thing as an education deduction for tax purposes. But under proper circumstances, education costs may be deducted as business expenses.

An executive is in the business of being an executive. An employee is in the business of being an employee. So any expenses necessary to do one's job or to hold one's job are deductible business expenses.

If the employer requires an employee to acquire certain education or to take particular courses *in order to keep his job,* the tuition is deductible, as are the costs of books, transportation, and the like. Example: a school engages a teacher, with the understanding that he can keep the job only if he acquires a master's degree within three years. Attaining the master's degree probably will mean a promotion and a higher salary. Expenses to qualify a person for a better job are not deductible, and such might have been the result of gaining an advanced academic degree. But here deduction is allowed because *maintenance* of the teacher's existing job was the immediate reason for taking the courses, even if later benefits reasonably could be expected. Another example is a person who is hired by an accounting firm, his continued employment being dependent upon his obtaining a certified public accountant's certificate. The cost of his courses of study is deductible because it was necessary to keep his present job.

An employee may deduct his education expenses if he can prove that his employer required study in prescribed areas in order to hold his job, designated subjects being in, for example, computer applications, foreign trade, taxation, or other fields associated with what the employer's work demanded. Proof of the right to the deduction can be furnished by a letter from one's superior insisting that specialized knowledge be acquired in order to keep the job. Alternatively, an employee could obtain a copy of his employer's job description specifications, which might show that further education was a prerequisite for the job. A board of education directive spelling out the essential need to acquire an advanced academic degree is an acceptable form of proof.

An attorney was permitted to deduct the cost of taking refresher courses in taxation, even though no one required him to do so, for he was not an employee. But he established the fact that his clients expected him to keep abreast of new developments in taxation, and he probably could not have retained his clients had he not done so. Taking the refresher courses was a way of keeping his existing clients.

In one case, a free-lance photographer was permitted to deduct the cost of flying lessons. He won his case by showing the court some actual examples of aerial photographs he had been able to take, which he could not have taken had he remained an earthbound photographer who could not get close to newsworthy events which he was enabled to snap as a result of being able to fly where the action was.

Employees' Expenses

An employee is able to deduct any expenses required by, or appropriate for, his business. A common example of this is the deduction of entertainment expenses for company customers, which ordinarily could be deducted only by the company itself, either directly or in the form of reimbursement to the employee making the actual outlay. But an executive or other employee may prefer to spend whatever amounts he thinks are necessary in order to get business, without restrictions imposed by his company's stingy habits or austerity program. He can deduct these expenses only if he is not entitled to reimbursement by the company. That can be arranged, either in the form of a letter or a directive in a company manual, as was illustrated in one case where an employee was permitted to deduct his costs of entertaining company customers:

"Mr. Luce and other Management officers have often emphasized that *TIME* salesmen are paid high salaries because selling is not a routine job and makes demands on a man's time and money that cannot be accounted for minute-by-minute or penny-by-penny. There are many expenses incidental to selling which the salesman is not expected to recover from the Company on top of his salary. In a very true sense, a salesman's job never ceases. And almost without exception his business life is closely interwoven with his personal social life. I make this point again because there are new men on the *TIME* staff who may never have heard of it. And because it explains why the Management does not expect an expense account to contain every phone call, every taxi ride, every luncheon, and every drink bought by a salesman in the course of his business and social existence." Fortunately, the taxpayer had saved a copy of his directive, which served as proof that he could deduct his expenses for entertaining company customers, for his employer expected him to do so without reimbursement by the company.

If a company employee goes to a convention, he must be able to prove that this was for business purposes rather than for a vacation or recreational jaunt. Otherwise, the Internal Revenue Service predictably will tax to him as additional compensation whatever the employer paid for his convention bills, either directly to the sponsoring organization or as reimbursement to him for out-of-pocket expenses. He can show that the convention was an appropriate business activity by retaining a copy of the agenda of meetings and seminars, assuming that they related to areas which benefitted him and the business. He may keep business notes which he took there, or assemble a list of the business contacts which he had made there.

Transactions Entered into for Profit

An individual cannot deduct expenses and losses of an activity unless it is a business or a transaction entered into for profit. If the activity is something which people generally enjoy doing, you have the burden of proving that your intention was to make money, even if for one reason or another that's not the way it worked out.

Here it is necessary to show that you had expectations of earning a profit. Proof of this may be established by showing that you consulted experts professionally before entering the activity, that you utilized the services of a knowledgeable accountant to see how your endeavors were working out, that you made efforts to eliminate unsuccessful operations and to replace them with something which appeared to be more promising, that you subscribed to trade and technical publications. In the case of a farm, which so often is a hobby rather than a business, it is helpful if you can show that there were no recreational facilities on the premises and that you engaged in physical endeavors which were so demanding that one would not have done that sort of thing for pleasure. If possible, have evidence as to why the endeavor had not been successful, such as a fire, the worst weather conditions in twenty years, serious illness.

Gambling Losses

The Internal Revenue Service has suggested to taxpayers how they could prove their gambling losses, which, if substantiated, are a proper offset against taxable gambling gains. Taxpayers are advised to keep a diary, containing at the very least this information:

1. Date and type of specific wager or wagering activities
2. Name of gambling establishment
3. Address or location of gambling establishment
4. Name(s) of other person(s), if any, present with the taxpayer at the gambling establishment
5. Amount(s) won and lost

The Service recommends that a person keep wagering tickets, cancelled checks, credit records, bank withdrawals. Other documentation could include hotel bills, airline tickets, gasoline credit cards, affidavits or testimony from responsible gambling officials regarding wagering activities.

Taxes

An individual should retain receipts for property taxes which he pays. When bills are paid by mail, state and local tax collectors frequently will issue receipted copies if the taxpayer includes with his check a stamped, self-addressed envelope. That is a worthwhile investment. If a bank or building and loan association has lent you money on a mortgage, it is a common practice for the financial institution to require you to make monthly payments of one-twelfth of the annual property tax, to be held in escrow until the actual property tax date comes around. In that event, you may not get a receipted copy of the tax bill, which may have been paid in installments. Retain the annual accounting you receive from the financial institution as proof that you have paid these taxes.

State and local sales taxes can amount to a respectable sum over the course of a year, but the chore of keeping seemingly endless pieces of paper is frightening in its magnitude: department store and other purchases, service stations, radio and television repair shops, and the like. The Internal Revenue Service has provided a substitute for this proof by itemization. Optional sales tax tables are published by the I.R.S., set up by state, providing a dollar amount which may be used without challenge by the Service, geared to each taxpayer's income and the number of persons in his family. If an individual elects to use the sales tax table, he is permitted to add to the amount shown the actual sales tax which he has paid in the case of automobiles, airplanes, boats, mobile homes, and materials used to build a new home when he is his own contractor. This means that the only bills and invoices which he has to retain as proof of the deduction are those for items listed in the previous sentence.

Capital Gains and Losses

Special information is necessary for the computation of capital gains and losses. Basically, there should be brokers' notifications or other written confirmations of all purchases of securities, regardless of *when* this took place. Similar information is required for sales. Acquisitions by gift, inheritance, or exchange should be noted, with contemporary documentation of the source of the figures.

As noted previously in this chapter, there should be retained the actual letters or advisory forms which were received along with the securities in the case of stock dividends, split-ups, spin-offs, exercise of rights and warrants, and corporate reorganizations.

There is no statute of limitations on the case of papers relating to the acquisition of capital assets, or other assets which are given comparable treatment for tax purposes.

Encouraging Other People to Be Pack Rats

In the case of property received by gift, the taxpayer's basis for determining gain or loss on disposition is whatever the donor paid for the property; or, if the donor himself received this property by gift, the last person who acquired it other than by gift. In order to establish this figure, it may be necessary to request the donor to turn over to you copies of invoice of purchases, regardless of how many years ago that was. If the donor received the property by inheritance from someone who died, the basis will be that used by the decedent's executor on the federal estate tax return. Should that estate have been too small to require the filing of a federal estate tax return, comparable information may be obtained from the forms filed for state death tax purposes.

Joint Ownership of Property

If a person is a co-owner of property with other persons, a time probably will come when it is necessary to establish the dollar extent of his interest. If he lacks the proper documentation, he is at the mercy of the Internal Revenue Service. For example, a person may be the co-owner of property with one or more other persons. When he dies, there is the practical question of how much of the jointly held property is considered to be part of his gross estate. The I.R.S. generally follows a rule of convenience: 100% of the value of jointly owned property is includible in a decedent's estate, unless his executor somehow can prove that the decedent's interest had been a lesser amount.

This calls for an unscrambling of the contributions made by each co-owner to the acquisition of the property, with adjustments for withdrawals or gifts since that time.

The same problem exists in the case of joint bank accounts and joint brokerage accounts.

In order to prove that *all* of the decedent's jointly held property is not taxable to his estate when he dies, efforts should be made right now to establish how much of such property really is the interest of one or more other co-owners.

Can Anyone Else Substantiate What's on Your Tax Return?

A generally overlooked problem of substantiation of what is on your federal income tax return is: Who is going to do it?

Even if you are confident that you can explain anything on the tax return to the satisfaction of a Revenue Agent, or that you can place your hands on any receipt or tax bill or any other document which is requested, it is extremely questionable whether anyone else could do so if you are not around to provide the answers. Obviously you cannot say that the problem will not be yours in that event. A person wants to leave as much as possible to his family or other beneficiaries. That amount can be vastly reduced if sizeable tax assessments are imposed against his estate because of items disallowed on his three final income tax returns solely because no one was able to explain what may have been perfectly correct figures.

Each taxpayer therefore should keep good workpapers with his copy of his income tax return, showing where the figures came from. Necessary supporting data in the form of brokers' memoranda, receipts, and the like should be attached, or there should be a statement about where this material can be found. Attach to your papers a page identifying your accountant, your lawyer, your broker. Where are your checkbooks?

A thoughtful person will attach to his will, or leave with his designated executor, a comparable statement of where everything is located which may prove to be useful in substantiating his income tax returns.

Show That You Had Relied on Competent Counsel

Ordinarily, a person can escape penalty for under-reported income if he can show that he had relied upon the advice of someone competent to advise him in tax matters, to whom a full disclosure of all of the facts had been made. But that time-honored defense could not be used in a 1980 case where an individual had chosen an attorney on the basis of his anti-tax sentiments, not because he was competent to provide sound tax advice.

6.
When You and the
Revenue Agent Can't Agree

When a federal income tax return is received by the Internal Revenue Service, the taxpayer's word—or arithmetic—is not taken for granted. There could be errors, unintentional or otherwise. Perhaps these are simple mathematical mistakes. Perhaps they are the result of a fiendishly clever fraud. According to a statement made by a Commissioner of Internal Revenue, "While audit activity is the primary method that the IRS uses to encourage voluntary compliance, every return is subject to scrutiny by IRS employees and computers."

Mathematical Verification

After a tax return is received at one of the I.R.S.'s ten service centers, it is first checked manually for completeness and accuracy and for such obvious errors as the claiming of a partial exemption or duplicate deductions. Then the service center's computers check the accuracy of the taxpayer's arithmetic and pick up other errors which may have escaped manual detection, such as the failure to reduce medical expense deductions by 3% of adjusted gross income.

If you wish to appeal the arithmetical corrections which the I.R.S. brings to your notice, this must be done within sixty days by sending the Service the reasons for the alleged non-agreement. This explanation must be sent with a copy of the notice which announced the figure correction. If your reasons are acceptable, the amount of tax change that was the result of the arithmetical error will be credited to your account and any overpayment will be refunded to you. If your reaons are not acceptable, you will be notified. Any remaining balance due the Service should be paid by the date shown on the notice in order to avoid any additional charges for interest or penalty. These appeal rights do not apply if the error occurred in the figuring of credits for federal income tax withheld, estimated tax payments, or the earned income credit.

During its 1979 fiscal year, the Internal Revenue Service checked the arithmetic on 90.6 million individual returns. Mathematical errors were found on 7.3% of these. On 3.8 million returns, tax liability was increased—an average of $241 per return. On 2 million returns, tax liability was decreased—an average of $159 per return.

Despite what many persons believe, the Service notifies taxpayers when mistakes are in their favor as well as when additional payments are due. This is done in the form of a computer print-out, on Form 4603. The taxpayer is informed, "This notice is not the result of an examination of your return. We notify the taxpayer when we select a return for examination." If tax has been overpaid, a refund check will be issued without need for formal application.

The I.R.S. service center review program generally is limited to the verification or resolution of issues which can be handled satisfactorily by service center personnel through correspondence with the taxpayer. Returns which call for a more intensive audit are sent to Internal Revenue Service district offices for completion.

Audit of Tax Returns

If a tax return is selected by the I.R.S. for examination, there will be either an office audit or a field audit. The former customarily involves returns with little or no business income and in general is confined to one or two items where further information may be needed. A field audit can cover anything related to the determination of a person's correct income tax liability. Office audits are conducted by Tax Auditors. Field examinations are handled by more thoroughly trained Revenue Agents.

No self-respecting business office likes to lose your account. And that goes for I.R.S. offices as well. When the Service undertakes to make an office audit of a federal income tax return, a taxpayer frequently requests that the examination be made at some Service office other than the one which is closest to his residence or business. Some I.R.S. offices balk at agreeing to this request, particularly if it is made at the request of the taxpayer's accountant or other representative who prefers to have the audit performed at a place more convenient for him. One office, in Newark, has announced that it no longer will transfer a case to another office unless there are unusual and/or special circumstances which affect the taxpayer rather than his representative. A request for a transfer to an office nearer the accountant or other representative, citing a desire to save the representative time and to minimize his fee, will be denied unless there are unusual circumstances such as a physical handicap or illness of the representative or the unavailability of pertinent books and records which cannot be transported conveniently.

If a person's only address is his home, or if the taxpayer is a business person working out of an office at home, there is where a field audit of his return ordinarily will take place, for that is where relevant records presumably are located. When a person is notified that his tax return is to be examined, he has the privilege of asking that this be done in his accountant's office, or his lawyer's, or some such place. This may be advisable if the taxpayer's home surroundings give the appearance of luxurious success, which could lead an impressionable Revenue Agent to conclude that income has been concealed if tax return figures do not look so impressive as the taxpayer's home. States the I.R.S. *Training Manual* supplied to Revenue Agents: "Taxpayer's standard of living is subject to observation. The agent should observe the neighborhood, furnishings, automobiles, etc. The quality of clothing worn by taxpayer and his family, as well as their shopping places and methods, should be noted. Their travel, entertainment and recreation styles are good barometers. The schools attended by their children afford another guide. The observant agent can draw a good picture of taxpayer's standard of living." And first impressions often are difficult to eradicate.

Some people buy anything an agreeable, persuasive salesman shows them. Know that it is stated in the Internal Revenue Manual prepared for the guidance of Revenue Agents that "ability as a salesman is an important qualification for an examination." So if your sales resistance is low, have a person of tougher fiber with you when confronted by a Revenue Agent.

Should You Be Represented by Counsel?

The answer to the question of representation by counsel during a federal tax conference really depends upon your own reactions to the situation. You do not have to bring counsel and you can always engage someone in the course of later developments if this seems to be indicated. Meanwhile, the amateur psychologists tell us, we may turn away suspicions because we aren't afraid to appear at a confrontation session without a lawyer or accountant. But that may be just what the Internal

Revenue Service is hoping that we will do. Says the I.R.S. *Training Manual:* "During the initial interview the taxpayer may answer more honestly, because he does not know why the questions are asked."

Your initial conference with a Revenue Agent can well determine what, if anything, comes next. Despite your knowledge of the tax requirements and your own confidence that you have met them, perhaps you don't come across well. The Service counsels its Revenue Agents in an office handbook: "The first symptoms alerting the agent to the possibility of fraud will frequently be provided by the taxpayer. His conduct during the examination . . . may be symptomatic of improper returns being filed." So if your basic honesty happens to be masked by the appearance and mannerisms of an old-fashioned Mississippi River steamboat gambler, it might be a good idea to be represented by a less beady-eyed type.

Sometimes it's better if a taxpayer appears only through a representative. One person claimed in court that he had been intimidated or threatened physically by a Revenue Agent. The court, in its own words, disbelieved him, "having seen Mr. Cioffi and the agent side by side."

Internal Revenue Service examiners are trained to do more than listen to your explanations. Examiners are admonished in the I.R.S. *Training Manual:* "Voice variations and facial expressions may indicate a need for more extensive questioning. Don't just hear the taxpayer's reply but observe his reaction. It may be more important than the answer." You should follow this suggestion, too. Watch the Revenue Agent's reactions to your story carefully, and if you don't like them, take time out and call in the troops.

That first conference may be the only one, so it is important to set the stage properly as to your own credibility and understanding of your obligations. It usually is a good idea not to volunteer anything but simply to answer whatever you are asked. Don't mention someone "high up" in the I.R.S. that you know very, very well. The Agent probably knows, or has access to, somebody who is even more highly placed.

One person sought court aid in preventing a bank from obeying an I.R.S. summons to produce whatever records it had in his name. These, if turned over to the Service, would amount to testifying against himself, he argued. And that would violate his Constitutional rights against self-incrimination. The court declined to interfere. He had not yet been charged with any crime, such as tax evasion, nor had he been requested to testify against himself.

The Fifth Amendment does not protect records an individual has turned over to his accountant from a government summons to the latter to disclose all of the taxpayer's records which he has. As the taxpayer voluntarily has surrendered possession of these papers, he no longer has a Constitutional right to safeguard them. How one taxpayer really had regarded his records, as indicated in a 1980 case, may have been revealed by the fact that he had delivered them to his accountant in garbage bags.

One person claimed that the government could not use against him in court an I.R.S. Certificate of Assessments and Payments which stated that he had filed no proper tax returns, until he had the right to confront his accuser. It was held in a 1980 decision that here the accuser could not be questioned, for the statement that the taxpayer hadn't filed any tax returns had come from a systematized data storage and retrieval system. This had to be regarded as trustworthy without having to have its memory jogged by cross-examination. You have no Constitutional right to confront a computer.

In general, you must show or produce for the examiner whatever he requests. But there are some exceptions to this requirement. In a criminal matter, such as tax fraud, the Fifth Amendment to the United States Constitution provides that no one can be compelled to testify against himself. But that does not mean that you can withhold anything which is required for the computation of correct taxable income. In a very real sense, any time you file a tax return, you are testifying against yourself. If the question arises as to whether the showing of records would tend to incriminate, it would be advisable to consult a lawyer who is versed in that tricky problem of what this Constitutional safeguard really means as applied to your particular situation. There are so many facets to this question that on a number of occasions the United States Supreme Court has had to interpret it.

Another area where you are not required to answer questions about your affairs or to produce records is where the question has nothing to do with your tax liability. Taxes are so intertwined with everything of a financial or business nature which we do that most matters in which you are involved could have tax implications. Some, of course, do not.

The Internal Revenue Service cannot demand information about matters which are protected by the ancient legal doctrine of *privilege*. In general, anything which passes between lawyer and client is privilege; that is, neither the government nor a court can compel either party to disclose what was discussed or to show papers which were part of the discussion. But privilege is very limited in its application. There is no privilege between a taxpayer and his accountant, or between a taxpayer and his bank. In 1972, the Supreme Court released new guidelines setting forth the rules of evidence to be used in federal courts. The privileged communications doctrine was extended to clergymen and to psychotherapists.

Unlike the attorney-client privilege, there is no accountant-client privilege. So the Internal Revenue Service can compel a taxpayer's accountant to disclose such items as opinions involving a client whose tax returns are being audited. This also covers tax planning and consulting papers. It is immaterial, said a court in a 1979 decision involving a major accounting firm, whether these papers actually were used in preparing tax returns if they relate in any way to the client's tax liability.

Likewise it is a mistake to think that whatever you discuss with a lawyer is confidential as far as the Internal Revenue Service is concerned. Privilege can be lost in a variety of situations. If anyone else is present during your discussion with a lawyer, the conversation loses its privilege. For example, you may ask your accountant to be present while you talk about a tax problem with an attorney. If you discuss a matter with your lawyer and a bank trust officer, the privilege is lost because someone else was present, even though, as often is the case, the trust officer also happens to be a lawyer. But he was not present in his capacity as a lawyer, being there rather in his role of trust officer. What is discussed with your lawyer is not privileged if he is not acting in his capacity as a lawyer. For example, many persons have their attorneys prepare tax returns for them. In such a situation, the lawyer really may be acting as an accountant and not as a lawyer. Persons frequently discuss financial problems with lawyers. If legal questions are not involved but merely investment or collection issues, what is discussed is not privileged. If you discuss a tax problem with a party who is both a lawyer and a certified public accountant, you have to prove precisely what was discussed with him in his role as attorney in order to keep it confidential. That is no slight problem.

Dealing with the Revenue Agent

"Tax collectors, and those who assist them," declared a judge in one decision, "have never been the objects of over-affection by the American Public." It is advisable, nonetheless, to remain on good, cordial terms with the Revenue Agent. Refusal to cooperate fully with him or her has been considered by courts to be equivalent to fraud, that is, willful attempt to evade taxes known to be due. Failure to keep appointments with a Revenue Agent or a pattern of stalling have been treated similarly.

Remember that most of what the Revenue Agent requests, he probably can get anyway if you fail to cooperate with him because of his power to have a subpoena or a summons issued. He may be able to get information from the other party to a transaction in which you were involved or from a bank which has records relating to it. Such tactics of resistance on your part can only poison the atmosphere of an audit and, if necessary, lead to the calling in of a tougher type of Revenue Agent who has had experience in coping with this sort of thing. You will not enjoy working with him.

Internal Revenue Service personnel don't win popularity awards. According to the *Annual Report of the Commissioner of Internal Revenue* in a recent year, 74% of all threats and 41% of all assaults on federal employees were directed at I.R.S. people.

If you show your teeth to a Revenue Agent, he can do more than bare his fangs. In one reported case, it was disclosed that an examiner was startled when a taxpayer took a close-up flashlight photograph of him while he was going over the taxpayer's records. The Agent then was told, "That's for posterity, so I can show it around and say 'this is the guy.' " Later, when the examiner asked the taxpayer for some records, the latter opened a desk drawer to reveal, not papers, but a cartridge box labeled "Smith & Wesson, .38 Chief Special." The taxpayer told the Revenue Agent that "there is no telling what he might not do if backed into a corner and there was no way out." A court held that this psychological warfare was an attempt to intimidate a federal employee. The cost: $3,000 fine, three months' imprisonment, nine months' probation.

The Internal Revenue Service, for its part, must adhere to certain ground rules. In the course of a tax audit, declares a manual prepared for Service personnel, "its agents must refrain from trickery, misrepresentation, or deception."

Before making a settlement with a government official, find out whether he can deliver. One person, charged with embezzlement of funds from a federal agency, plea-bargained with an assistant U.S. attorney. The person insisted that in return for a plea of guilty to this charge, he was promised immunity from assessment and collection of taxes by the I.R.S. Whether such a bargain ever had been made, who knows? But the assistant U.S. attorney had no legal right to make such an agreement. And, noted the court in a 1980 decision, a party entering into an agreement with a representative of the U.S. has the responsibility of finding out the bounds of that representative's authority.

A person may plead guilty to a state charge involving the taking of money when the state prosecutor promises that the I.R.S. won't be informed. In one case, the state prosecutor even threw in the helpful intelligence that his brother-in-law was a local I.R.S. agent. But the Service was permitted to get involved anyway after it was clued in by the state. An unauthorized party, regardless of his state title and position, can't bind federal authorities to forgo prosecution.

Authorization or Representation

If, at any time during the audit or appeals process, a taxpayer wishes to be represented by an attorney or anyone else, the former should sign Form 2848, "Power of Attorney," or Form 2848–D, "Authorization and Declaration."

Only a lawyer or other person licensed to practice before the Internal Revenue Service can *represent* a taxpayer before the Service. But anyone in possession of relevant facts may appear as a witness. Some professional tax preparers, as part of their service, offer to accompany a client when his return is being audited by the I.R.S., not as a legal representative, but merely to explain how the figures on the tax return were derived.

The Assessment Process

After a Revenue Agent completes his examination, he writes up a report, which is reviewed by his group manager. The report then goes to the Review Staff of the Audit Division, which may reject proposed assessments or ask for further investigations. After this, the Revenue Agent's report is sent to the taxpayer. If he agrees with the findings, he is asked to sign Form 870, which is an acceptance of the tax assessment or notice of overassessment. The taxpayer's signing of this form does not finalize the Revenue Agent's report. Either the taxpayer or the Internal Revenue Service later can repudiate it. The purpose of a taxpayer's signing this form is to stop the running of interest thirty days after the form is signed, even if the actual processing of the formal deficiency notice (the bill) takes a considerable length of time. But a taxpayer, even after he has signed Form 870, still may be assessed tax on additional items.

If a taxpayer disagrees with the Revenue Agent's report, it is given a technical review by the Review Staff at the District Director's office. Should this staff see no objection, the taxpayer is sent a communication on Form L–87, which states that if he does not notify the I.R.S. of what he intends to do about the disagreement within thirty days, a bill will be issued in line with the Revenue Agent's report.

The Internal Revenue Service encourages the resolution of tax disputes through an administrative appeals system rather than litigation. Taxpayers who disagree with a proposed change in their tax liability are entitled to a prompt, independent review of their cases. This is designed to minimize taxpayer inconvenience, expense, and delay in the disposition of contested cases. Most differences, the I.R.S. has stated, can be settled through an appeal to higher authority within the Service without expensive and time-consuming litigation.

Until recently, disputes were argued out in the local district offices of the I.R.S., with appeals then being heard by an appellate division in each of the seven Service regions. This duplication of hearings was simplified, beginning in October 1978. A Regional Director of Appeals now is in charge of all appeals for his district. He or she also handles disputes which had been appealed to the Examination and Collections Divisions at district conferences. But a taxpayer will not have to travel to the Regional Director's office, which may be in a distant city; conferences still are being held in each district office, as in the past.

The appeals process within the I.R.S. is conducted informally. Taxpayers may represent themselves or be represented by a professional person who is enrolled to practice before the Service. According to the report of the Commissioner of Internal Revenue for the fiscal year 1978, 97% of all disputed cases in the past ten years were closed without going to the courts.

Failure of an I.R.S. official to reject a settlement made at a lower level doesn't mean it was approved. In an effort to settle taxpayer disputes, the Service has designated various appeals officers. Internal procedures may require that an appeals officer's settlements be approved by a person at a higher level. Approval of a written agreement made by a taxpayer and an I.R.S. appeals officer cannot be inferred simply because the higher level authority had failed to repudiate the settlement, declared a 1980 decision. Here a mutually acceptable written agreement made by taxpayer and appeals officer was disregarded simply because no higher echelon person had gotten around to approving it.

As a taxpayer appeals his controversy to successively higher levels within the Service, he will at each stage encounter persons with greater tax sophistication and experience. This could lead to the imposition of additional tax on items which the Revenue Agent had overlooked, for a tax review is not limited to items picked up during the original audit. Some tax practitioners believe that a settlement should be reached by the taxpayer at the lowest level in order to prevent the raising of additional issues by more knowledgeable I.R.S. persons. In addition, the higher the appeal goes, the more technical is the approach of the Service representative likely to be, which puts at a disadvantage a taxpayer who is unfamiliar with rules and procedures.

Problem Resolution Program

Sometimes it seems to be impossible to get anywhere through normal channels in The System. Under the Problem Resolution Program (PRP), the Internal Revenue Service attempts to resolve taxpayers' complaints not satisfied through normal processes and, in the long run, to identify systematic and procedural problems that need correcting. If you have a problem with the Service and have tried without success to get it resolved through regular assistance activities, call the I.R.S.'s toll-free telephone number for your area listed in the telephone directory under "U.S. Government—Internal Revenue Service" and ask for the Problem Resolution Office. Although this office isn't a substitute for normal Service channels and cannot change technical decisions or interfere with an examination, often it is able to help taxpayers to clear up misunderstandings which have resulted from previous contact with the Service.

During 1979, about 72 thousand taxpayer problems were resolved through PRP, where satisfaction had not been obtained through normal channels.

Appeals to the Courts

If a taxpayer cannot obtain a satisfactory settlement of his dispute in the appeals process within the I.R.S., he will be sent a statutory notice of deficiency, known as a "ninety-day letter," which finalizes the assessment but gives him ninety days in which to petition the United States Tax Court to review his case. (The time is one hundred and fifty days where the taxpayer's address is outside of the United States.) If this petition is filed on time, the Tax Court will set up the case for trial at a location which is convenient to the taxpayer. He may represent himself or he may be represented by anyone admitted to practice before that court.

Where the disputed tax is $5,000 or less for any taxable year, there is a simplified procedure available under the Tax Court's small case rules. At little cost in time or money, a taxpayer can present his own case for a binding decision which is final and cannot be appealed. A streamlined form of petition for such a trial is submitted on T.C. Form 2 to the Tax

Court within ninety days of the date appearing on the deficiency notice, with a $10 filing fee. The taxpayer describes on this form why he thinks the I.R.S. was in error in assessing him, and in which of about fourscore possible cities he would like to have his case heard. Write for information about the Small Tax Case procedure to the United States Tax Court, 400 Second Street, Washington, D.C. 20217.

But, as a 1980 decision shows, a decision under this procedure cannot be appealed to a higher court. One strike and you're out if you use the small tax case procedure.

A typographical error on your letterhead can forfeit your right to use the Tax Court. A person's request for a Tax Court review may be too late if he does not receive his notice of deficiency from the I.R.S. in time to respond within ninety days. One individual wrote several letters to the Service while his audit was in process, and the deficiency notice was sent to the address on his letterhead. But that had been imprinted with an incorrect zip code number. By the time the letter did reach him, the ninety days had passed. So had his right to a Tax Court review, it was held in a 1981 decision.

If you litigate the same type of item too frequently in the Tax Court, that tribunal can show its disapproval. After disallowing the item, the court can assess its own penalty of up to $500 on the ground that the litigation was merely to delay the payment of taxes. And that is not all that can happen. Claiming a deduction of a type which was disallowed on a prior audit can result in having a fraud penalty imposed by the Internal Revenue Service for willfully seeking to evade taxes known to be due, because by now you know that your tax is not reduceable by this item. That's what happened in a 1980 case where a taxpayer asked the court to review an issue which that tribunal already had rejected three times in previous years.

Appeals

Whichever party, taxpayer or I.R.S., loses in the Tax Court can appeal within a set time to one of ten courts of appeals, according to geographical location. As noted previously, this appeals procedure is not available where the small tax case procedure of the Tax Court has been used. Rarely does a taxpayer, other than a lawyer experienced in this particular area, represent himself in a court of appeals, for it may be impossible to correct any procedural error which is made at this level. Whoever loses there can apply to the United States Supreme Court for a further hearing, although it is optional for the top tribunal to accept the case. (The party who loudly proclaims that "I'll take this to the Supreme Court" either does not know what he is talking about or is orating for the record, as nobody takes a case to that court unless it chooses to accept it.) If appeal is not made to the Supreme Court within the permitted time, or if that body declines to review the case, the court of appeals decision is final. The amount of any tax deficiency, to the extent that it has not been whittled down by a court, now must be paid, with interest.

Rather than go to the Tax Court, thereby suspending payment of tax until that court's decision is rendered and becomes final, a taxpayer may pay the tax demanded by the I.R.S., file a refund claim for its recovery with the Service, and, when that claim is rejected as predictably it will be, sue for a refund in a federal district court. This suit also may be filed if the I.R.S. has not acted upon the refund claim for six months. The advantage of suing for a refund in the district court is that tax already has been paid and hence interest is limited if you get nowhere in court. But an even greater advantage in many instances is that when you sue for a refund in a district court, you have a right to request a jury trial. A jury is likely to contain some businesspersons. Very frequently, they have a strong bias against the Internal Revenue Service or, for that matter, against any other governmental body which seems to be telling someone how to run his affairs. For example, if a taxpayer has been disallowed a deduction because of some technicality, or where a matter of judgment was involved, the businessperson-juror may think, "If I let the government get away with this, next time *I* may be the one who is penalized because I did not understand, or could not comply with, some stupid bureaucratic red tape."

Whoever loses in the district court can go to the court of appeals, as previously described.

Alternately, a taxpayer can sue for his tax refund in the Court of Claims. This differs from the district court procedure in that appeals can go only to the Supreme Court—if it wants to accept the case. If it does not, the decision of the Court of Claims is final.

Sometimes a taxpayer wants to get his case before a court quickly. He may feel that agreement or settlement with the Internal Revenue Service just is not possible. For example, he may believe that the amounts involved are so large or his arguments are so novel that no I.R.S. representative will stick his chin out. Perhaps the Service attitude in matters of this sort in the past has been completely unyielding. So where speedy court action is desired, the taxpayer can pay the asserted deficiency, file a claim for refund, and then request in writing that the claim be rejected immediately. The I.R.S. will be happy to oblige. A notice of disallowance will be sent to him promptly, at which time he can at once file suit for recovery of his money in the appropriate district court. This could save him six months' time.

How Does the Taxpayer Fare in the Various Courts?

If you and the Internal Revenue Service cannot work out a settlement to your liking and it's necessary to let a court decide the issue(s), what tribunal looks to be the most attractive? If you lose there and are considering an appeal to a higher court, what do the statistics indicate as to your chances? The following helpful data are for the government's 1979 fiscal year.

	TAXPAYER WON	I.R.S. WON	SPLIT DECISIONS
Trial Court Record			
Tax Court	9.9%	52.5%	37.6%
District Court	28.5%	60.3%	11.2%
Court of Claims	37.5%	50.0%	12.5%
Appellate Court Record			
Court of Appeals	18.0%	76.2%	5.8%
Supreme Court	66.7%	33.3%	—

When a Taxpayer's Records Are Useless for Audit

The customary federal income tax audit involves verification of the figures on a return, or at least a test of their adequacy. But at times the I.R.S. will conclude that taxpayer's records simply do not substantiate what appears on the tax return. Then the Service is authorized to reconstruct taxable income upon the basis of the best evidence which is available or procurable. This can happen in the case of fraud, where relevant data are concealed or destroyed. But it also can happen where a person merely did not understand the need to keep reliable records. Or he may have been so careless or sloppy that the records were utterly unreliable.

The Internal Revenue Service has a variety of methods for the reconstruction of a person's taxable income. One of the most frequently applied techniques is the *net worth method*. This may be used even where all of the transactions with tax significance appear upon one's books and records. In the words of one court, "a showing of unrecorded items is not prerequisite to the use of this method of reconstruction of income."

In order to reconstruct a taxpayer's income under this method, the I.R.S. must show (1) the lack of adequate records, (2) the beginning and ending net worth of the taxpayer for each year involved in the audit, and (3) a likely source of income which would be taxable. The Service then takes the increase in net worth, adds on the taxpayer's non-deductible expenditures such as living expenses, and characterizes any excess of this adjusted net worth increase over reported taxable income as unreported taxable income. Although originally the I.R.S. used the net worth method only in the case of hardened criminals, now the technique is applied even in the case of "respectable types," such as legitimate businesspersons, physicians, judges, and clergymen. In the picturesque words of one decision, "Using 'net worth statements' to demonstrate an unexplained flowering of taxpayer's wealth, the government sought to show that the luxuriating of financial seedlings into larger plants were attributable to the receipts of unreported monetary nutrients."

For example, an individual operates a retail store. Most of his receipts are in the form of cash, but daily adding machine tapes were not preserved, nor was there any independent verification of the figures shown on the federal income tax return nor reconciliation with nonexistent books. Clearly the records were inadequate; and if an increase in net worth can be shown by the I.R.S. for a taxable year, the Service is allowed to reconstruct income by pointing out the obvious fact that a retail establishment certainly has ways of generating income.

The I.R.S. may impose tax on the amount you're simply assumed to have spent. For example, if a person is addicted to the use of drugs, the cost of his habit must have come from somewhere. In a 1980 case where a person admittedly was an addict in 1974, but had little reported income in 1973, the I.R.S. sought to tax him on unreported income for that year in an amount equal to $50 a day for drugs times 365, or $18,250 to sustain the habit for a year. He won his tax case by convincing the court he hadn't been a drug addict for that year.

But the Service must follow up leads furnished by the taxpayer as to the existence of non-taxable receipts which might have accounted for any increase in net worth. With its vast investigatory powers, the I.R.S. may be able to verify that the taxpayer had indeed received a substantial gift in cash when his mother from Central Europe had paid him a visit that year. The taxpayer has the opportunity of showing the non-existence of all possible sources of taxable income, such as where he had been institutionalized during the entire taxable year or had been a prisoner of war.

In one case, a physician stated that he had gotten $200,000 in new $100 bills from his ninety-two-year old father in Germany, a long-time baker. But his story about getting the "dough" from his father the baker during a vacation trip could not be verified, for the doctor had failed to bring to the attention of customs officers upon return to his country an alleged four envelopes, each two inches thick, which he said had been on his person.

Where the Internal Revenue Service determines a person's income under the net worth method, he is not entitled under the Freedom of Information Act to see the Service's files dealing with the reconstruction.

Another technique used by the I.R.S. to reconstruct a taxpayer's income is the *bank deposit method*. Unexplained deposits are regarded as having been unreported taxable income. It is up to the taxpayer to establish what the deposits represented, although the Service is required to use its inquisitorial forces to try to run down his clues as to undocumented inflows of cash. In one case, an individual claimed that he had obtained $75,355 in currency in a box in his father's apartment when the parent died. The Service dutifully investigated this lead, but it proved to be of no benefit to the taxpayer. It was determined that the father had earned only $30,000 during his last twenty-three years, that no estate had been administered, and that no New York estate tax return had been filed.

A 1979 decision shows that available facts can establish nontaxability even when a taxpayer no longer can. Shortly before his death, a physician had banked a six-figure amount in cash. Logically enough, the I.R.S. thought that this was simply another case where a doctor took cash fees from patients without bothering to record the transactions and to pay taxes on them. But the seventy-four-year-old physician had been virtually retired because of his many infirmities for thirteen years, seeing only a few longtime patients in his home. He appeared to have been too ill to have engaged in illegal or other income-producing activities. During his many high production years, he had reported considerable income from his practice and hence could have accumulated a sizeable hoard. The bank deposits were made after his home had been burglarized twice; on one occasion, he had been robbed at gun point. Fortunately for the taxpayer, he had reported to the police these stick-ups, which had taken place shortly before the bank deposits. Fear of further heists was an acceptable reason for the unexplained deposits.

Also used by the I.R.S. is the *cash expenditure method*. The net worth method is not effective in the case of a person who channels his unreported income into investments or realty, apparently winding up a year no wealthier than he had been at the start of the period. The cash expenditure method was devised to reach such a person by establishing the amount of his purchases of goods and services which are not attributable to the resources on hand at the beginning of the year or to non-taxable receipts during the year.

Under the *source and application of funds method,* the Internal Revenue Service determines the minimum amount of cash expenditures made by a person in the taxable years and, after deducting all cash available to him from known sources, concludes that the remainder of the cash he spent in those years represented unreported income.

Other methods are used by the Service in the absence of records, or of records which can be believed. For example, in the case of a merchant, the cost of inventories is estimated, and an assumed markup is applied to produce a figure which supposedly represents taxable profit.

Under all of these reconstruction methods, a taxpayer can be hurt by coincidences or just plain poor memory or failure of proof. For example, maybe he really did find a large cash hoard in a sofa which he had purchased from an itinerant junk dealer. But in the absence of proof, such as an immediate report to the police, he will be taxed. The courts have held that reconstructed income for this purpose need not be computed with mathematical certainty.

I.R.S. Not Responsible for Overzealous Acts of Its Agents

The audit of federal income tax returns and the collection of taxes are not always carried on in sweet harmony. The taxpayer or the Revenue Agent, or both, may behave unreasonably and in contemptuous disregard of the legitimate interests of the other party. When a taxpayer refuses to behave as he is required to do, the I.R.S. has ways of showing its teeth. Sometimes this is very expensive to the taxpayer and actually was not justified in the first place. But the taxpayer cannot sue the Internal Revenue Service even for the monetary damage he has sustained, such as where another party actually was the one who owed back taxes which the Service proceeded to collect through heroic measures. One cannot sue the government without its consent, and the I.R.S. is a governmental agency. It is immune to suit without its consent, which is not freely given.

Here is an actual case: When a contractor failed to hire union labor, the union threatened that he could anticipate a visit from the Internal

Revenue Service. An examiner came around as predicted. Then the Service claimed that the business owed back taxes for depreciation taken on its buildings. During the course of its investigation and collection activities, the I.R.S. told the firm's creditors of alleged tax violations and said the outfit would become insolvent as a result of what was going to happen. Consequently, credits dried up, and the taxpayer was forced out of business. The Service, furthermore, harassed and intimidated the taxpayer and his wife in its collection activities, and on several occasions seized and attached property belonging to them. After several years of audit and investigation, the I.R.S. determined that no taxes really were owed, and returned $6,500 which had been collected by various seizures. The taxpayer brought suit against the United States. In helpless frustration, the court threw up its figurative hands, the judge muttering something about "deplorable." But the suit was dismissed, for the government had not given its consent to be sued. The Federal Tort Claims Act does not permit the government to use this defense where the claimant has been injured, such as here. But the act does not apply when the damage was sustained in connection with the assessment or collection of taxes.

Such was also the result in a case in which a taxpayer's property in Westchester County, New York, was seized by the United States to satisfy a tax lien in favor of the government for taxes which actually were owed by somebody else. (A lien is the right to retain possession of property until a debt is paid.) Although the government was in possession of his property for only six weeks before it was discovered that the tax liability was another party's, the property was returned to him in badly damaged condition. He argued that the United States had not protected his belongings adequately to prevent damage from a tropical storm which had occurred during this period, despite ample warning of the danger. Then there was the matter of lost rents and profits from the buildings which never should have been seized. But the government did not consent to be sued, claiming that all of this resulted from its sincere attempt to collect taxes, which, unfortunately, happened to be owed by another taxpayer.

A taxpayer was behind in his federal tax payments. As permitted by law, the I.R.S. seized some of the taxpayer's assets and sold them for back taxes. Claiming that the Service maliciously sold these properties well below fair market value, thus ruining the business, the taxpayer sued the United States for alleged misconduct of the Revenue Agents involved. Although the Federal Tort Claims Act permits action to be brought against the U.S. for certain wrongful acts, an exception is made where, as here, the claim arises in connection with the assessment and collection of taxes.

One taxpayer sued a Revenue Agent and the Government on the ground that his tax audit had been conducted maliciously with a view to causing injury. It was claimed that the Agent didn't like the nature of the taxpayer's business, which involved services to Medicaid patients, and that this examiner had threatened to reopen an earlier investigation if the taxpayer refused to agree to deficiencies now being proposed. Even if that threat had been made in bad faith, ruled the court in a 1980 decision, competent counsel could have been engaged to respond to any prosecutorial persuasion and false condemnation. So the taxpayer didn't need, or get, help from the court.

A bankrupt corporation was for sale. One person offered to buy it for $35,000, if he could have assurances that that was all he would have to pay. Trade creditors, whose accounts receivable were settled in the receivership proceedings, had no further claims. The I.R.S. had a tax claim for a specified amount, which had been provided for in the bankruptcy proceedings, and the Service declared that this claim covered everything. Later, however, the new buyer was called upon to make further tax payments which were said to be due by the corporation he had acquired. But you said nothing additional was owed, or I wouldn't have bought the company, cried the purchaser. Declared a 1980 decision: ''While it is true that agents of the I.R.S. frequently misrepresent matters to taxpayers, all of which create a 'credibility gap' that tends to make them not worthy of belief and works a great deal of hardship on taxpayers, and while it would appear that when a person appears in court and consents to an action that he should be bound thereby, Congress has nevertheless seen fit to exclude I.R.S. from the law and to specifically permit misrepresentation on the part of the agent.''

Duress

A signed agreement with the I.R.S. is not binding upon a taxpayer if he has signed under duress or coercion. One person had a disagreement with the Revenue Agent shortly before the three-year statute of limitation would have prevented further action by the Service. The taxpayer was told that unless he signed an agreement extending the length of time during which the tax return remained open for further action, the tax would be assessed at once and he would lose his right to appeal to a higher

I.R.S. official. The taxpayer signed. Later he claimed that he had done so under duress, in order not to lose his right of further appeal within the Service. A 1980 decision held that the Agent had the right to threaten to assess tax without opportunity for this appeal to a higher level if the agreement wasn't signed before the statute of limitation expired. The assertion of an intention to pursue a proper legal process isn't duress.

Personal Immunity of Revenue Agents

If a conscientious Revenue Agent fears that angry taxpayers will bring suit against him for real or imaginary damages, he may hesitate to be sufficiently aggressive in enforcing the tax laws. So a Revenue Agent is exempt from suit if his acts, in the words of one court decision, have "more or less connection with the general matters committed by law to his control or supervision." That gives a Revenue Agent a startling amount of leeway, for his authority is very broad. Innocent persons hurt by his overzealousness may not hold him accountable.

One individual's bank account was attached by the Internal Revenue Service for unpaid taxes. (An attachment is the seizure of property by lawful authority for debts.) Later a court held that the attachment was improper, for she was not the one who really owed these taxes. She brought suit against the I.R.S. employees who had deprived her of her sizeable bank account, claiming that these persons had acted maliciously and in disregard of her rights, for they knew or should have known that she was not the debtor. She had suffered genuine costs and losses. She engaged counsel to try to prevent the attachment; she sustained losses because of the need to sell other property to raise money for the lawyer. But she could get no satisfaction for all of this, for the I.R.S. persons, although they had been in error and may have acted maliciously, were performing within the wide scope of their authority.

Another individual had his bank account attached because of nonpayment of taxes, which actually he had paid. As a result, checks he had drawn on his account were returned by reason of "Insufficient Funds." A notice of levy (collection by legal process) was served on his employer, so that part of his salary would be paid directly to the government. Three months after his bank account was attached, he got back his money. He brought suit against the collection officer seeking damages for defamation of character, malicious prosecution, deprivation of individual rights, and negligence. It was held that the I.R.S. official was immune from civil suit while acting within the scope of his authority and in discharge of his regular duties, even though the acts were completely unjustified, inasmuch as no taxes were owed, and that was a matter of record. Meanwhile, the taxpayer had to live with the fact that people knew some of his checks had bounced, and his employer had been told officially that he was a tax deadbeat.

One person's property was seized by the Internal Revenue Service because allegedly he owed taxes on a transaction, the taxability of which was being argued through proper channels elsewhere. He brought suit against the I.R.S. personnel who had seized the property, claiming that he could not sell his property while the lien was on it and that he had suffered economic and character injuries because of the implication that he was financially unable or personally unwilling to pay taxes, even though his property had been taken before any court even had heard arguments as to whether he really owed any taxes at the time. His suit was dismissed by the court.

In a credit-oriented economy, there are few things more harmful to a person than unfavorable input into his credit records and rating. Where one person's property was subjected to a lien for unpaid federal income taxes, he claimed that he had been subjected to unnecessary, substantial, and permanent damage in a malicious way. Maybe so, declared the court in a 1980 decision. But the I.R.S. representative was only acting within the bounds of her authority.

One taxpayer sought to sue a Revenue Agent for violation of civil rights on two grounds: (1) the Agent had threatened that if the taxpayer appealed the proposed deficiency, his case would be referred to the Intelligence Division for possible criminal prosecution, and (2) the Agent had harassed the taxpayer's bank by requesting so many unnecessary records that the desperate bank finally terminated its financing arrangements with the taxpayer. The court rejected the action on both grounds. As to (1), declared the court, "bargaining with the taxpayer in an effort to reach agreement on the amount of a deficiency is an accepted I.R.S. tactic." As to (2), a taxpayer doesn't have a Constitutional right "to a financing arrangement with one's bank free from interference from a government agent."

A taxpayer may complain of harassment by examiners. But, declared one judge, "This Court will not normally look behind the deficiency notice to examine into the manner in which the agents of the Internal Revenue Service have conducted themselves."

Still virtually untested is the effect of a United States Supreme Court decision in 1974. This held that a government employee's immunity from suit exists only if (1) at the time and in the light of all the circumstances there existed reasonable grounds for the belief that his action was proper and (2) the employee acted in good faith.

Taxpayer May Be Reimbursed for Legal Fees

In order to deter the government from using tax proceedings to harass or to intimidate taxpayers, Congress permitted such persons to recover the cost of defending themselves against unwarranted claims. The Civil Rights Attorney's Fees Award Act of 1976 provides that courts may award a reasonable part of legal fees expended to taxpayers who successfully defend themselves against the Internal Revenue Service in court. This law was characterized as a beginning attempt to penalize oppressive governmental action which imposes unreasonable expenses upon a taxpayer. That a claim was unwarranted is established when the taxpayer wins in court. He cannot be the one who instituted the proceedings; he must have been the defendant to be entitled to recovery of any part of his costs. But where one taxpayer filed a refund claim and the I.R.S. retaliated by filing a counterclaim against her, she became a defendant and, when she won her right to refund in court, she could be reimbursed for her legal fees.

A corporation failed to turn over to the I.R.S. the amounts deducted from employee paychecks as withholding taxes. The Service sued the "responsible parties" *personally* for these sums, naming the president-treasurer and the bookkeeper. The government admitted that it had sued the bookkeeper, who had a modest salary and was not a shareholder, only so that she would testify in great detail against the president, who was the real target of the I.R.S. But inasmuch as she had to hire a lawyer because of the government's bad faith in using her as a cat's paw to catch someone else, she was entitled to collect legal fees from the U.S.

An individual also was entitled to collect his legal fees from the government in a 1980 case where, after a dispute where he actually was correct according to facts in the I.R.S.'s possession, the Service posted a lien against his property and demanded an amount far larger than the Service believed to be due, admittedly as an "attention-getter" or bargaining wedge.

A do-it-yourself taxpayer is not entitled to collect attorneys' fees even where the I.R.S. was in error. If he tries his own case, there has been no attorney whose fees could be reimbursable.

There is no entitlement to any reimbursement of legal fees, however, where the government has appealed a lower court's decision in favor of the taxpayer if no harassment of the taxpayer or bad faith was involved.

On occasion, a taxpayer may have to pay the government's legal fees. After one person had gone to court six times on matters which various tribunals had considered to be without merit, a court issued an injunction which forbade him to file any further actions related to his past federal tax liabilities. Then he was warned that further tying up the I.R.S.'s time would result in a bill for attorneys' fees.

The Equal Access to Justice Act

The Equal Access to Justice Act, which took effect on October 1, 1981, provides that when an individual, partnership, or corporation has had to incur expenses in order to vindicate its rights against action by the U.S. which was not substantially justified, an award will be made to cover lawyers' fees, expert witnesses' charges, and other costs. This redress is not available to an individual whose net worth exceeded $1,000,000 when the action was filed, or to the sole owner of an unincorporated business or a partnership, corporation, or other organization whose net worth exceeded $5,000,000.

Right to Free Tax Counsel

If a person is charged with the crime of tax evasion, he is entitled to counsel, which will be supplied by the court without charge to a needy taxpayer. But he must prove that he cannot afford to pay for his own defense. In a United States District Court, a party seeking cost-free legal representation must list his assets, liabilities, and employment on a standard questionnaire, Form CJA–23. One alleged tax delinquent refused to answer questions about his resources on the ground that this would amount to testifying against himself. The judge replied that he alone would see any figures submitted but, without them, he could not appoint costless counsel. The taxpayer continued to refuse. So did the judge.

Compromise of Taxes

If a person is financially unable to pay his federal income taxes in full, he may submit an offer in compromise application, Form 656, to the Service. This must be accompanied by Form 433, "Statement of Financial Condition and Other Information." One individual filed such a statement of financial condition on February 13, "as of" January 30, listing assets of what amounted to petty cash. But on February 5, he actually had received Federal Reserve checks for $30,000 which went unmentioned on the statement. So the statement on the basis of which he had been granted a reduction in taxes owed was incorrect, and the compromise deal was cancelled. In addition, he was jailed for having made a false statement to the Internal Revenue Service.

The Internal Revenue Service may be willing to compromise a tax liability on either of two grounds: (1) doubt as to liability, or (2) doubt as to collectibility. The amount acceptable by the Service in the case of (1) depends upon the degree of doubt found in a particular situation as to the facts or correct treatment. In the case of (2), an acceptable offer must reflect all that can be collected from a taxpayer's income, present or prospective, after giving effect to all priorities such as liens granted to the government. Here an agreement may be required as to payments from future income and, where applicable, to the relinquishment of certain present or potential tax benefits. Public inspection of any offer in compromise accepted by the government is authorized. That could subject a taxpayer to blackmail if he tried to conceal income or assets.

It takes two parties to make a tax compromise. One individual, upon receipt of a tax deficiency notice for $2,896.83, countered with a check for $500 in compromise of the bill. He wrote on the check, "1972 Tax Audit Returns Paid in Full." He was notified that the settlement proposal was unacceptable, but the Service deposited his check anyway, applying it against the unpaid account. When a bill for the balance came in, he argued indignantly that the matter had been settled by compromise. The court ruled otherwise. The Internal Revenue Service, by depositing a check, is not bound by what a taxpayer has chosen to write on it, even though other creditors may be bound when they deposit such a check.

Income from discharge of indebtedness in compromise with the Internal Revenue Service is taxable.

Compromise of Issues or Values

When a taxpayer and the I.R.S. cannot agree upon the proper tax treatment of a controversial question, usually the parties leave the hassle to a court to decide. With increasing frequency, judges are advising the parties to swap horses, for a dispute, in the words of one court, may be "more susceptible of negotiation and settlement than being subjected to the legal process . . ." In one 1980 decision, the judge advised, "Our wish is always that cases such as this be settled." In another case decided that same day, the judge declared that he did not agree with either party. His decision may have displeased both of them, although their own compromise might have satisfied both parties.

Before you litigate, note what the judge declared in a 1980 decision: "Cases brought under the Income Tax laws of this country are at best confusing and at worst beyond understanding."

Second Examination

The I.R.S. is not entitled to a second look at a taxpayer's records, unless the District Director of Internal Revenue notifies him in writing that a second inspection is necessary. A Revenue Agent is unlikely to ask his superior to write such a letter if this might indicate that the original examination had been careless, so the matter may end there. Or through administrative foul-ups the District Director may not have written the letter and hence no second examination can be made. But it was ruled in 1980 that one taxpayer couldn't argue that a new request to see his records was a *second* examination without formal demand by the District Director, because there was nothing to indicate that the *first* one had ever been completed. Actually the audit had revealed that there was nothing to change, so the Agent stopped at that point. His failure to write "no change" meant that the re-inspection by another person wouldn't have been a second examination.

How to Avoid Repetitive Audits

Sometimes a person feels that he is on the Internal Revenue Service "hit list." Every year his federal income tax return is selected for audit. If he is questioned about certain items on his return, and these same issues have been raised in either of the two preceding years with little or no change in his tax liability, he can reply to the initial contact letter from the Service in the year when this point is raised again, advising the I.R.S. of the facts. Copies of the initial contact letters of previous years involving the same point should be attached to his reply. This procedure applies only to individuals, not corporations.

If the issues are similar *and no other compelling reasons exist* for examining the return, the audit will be terminated and the taxpayer so notified. The meaning of the italicized words is purposely vague.

Closing Agreements

It was mentioned earlier in this chapter that despite what many persons believe, the signing of a Form 870 by a taxpayer, consenting to an assessment or overassessment of tax, does not prevent either the taxpayer or the Internal Revenue Service from reopening a taxable year if the statute of limitations has not run out.

But a *closing agreement,* except as noted subsequently, means what it says. Such an agreement is available only where there appears to be an advantage (to the Internal Revenue Service) in having a case permanently and conclusively closed, or if good and sufficient reasons are shown by a taxpayer for desiring a closing agreement and it is determined by the I.R.S. that the government will sustain no disadvantage through the making of such an agreement.

If a closing agreement is made, this usually takes place directly after the completion of a tax audit. It may determine total tax liability of a taxpayer for specific taxable periods, or it may refer to agreement on specified facts. For this purpose, both the taxpayer and the Internal Revenue Service must sign the appropriate document: Form 866, "Agreement as to Final Determination of Tax Liability," or Form 906, "Closing Agreement as to Final Determination Covering Specific Matters."

The I.R.S. may set aside such a signed agreement if it was obtained through fraud or through the misrepresentation by the taxpayer of a material fact.

A closing agreement may be useful in such instances as these:

1. To establish tax liability so that a transaction may be facilitated, such as the sale of stock

2. To wind up such affairs as liquidation of a business or settlement of an estate, or division of property of spouses incident to a divorce

3. To satisfy creditors' demands for authentic evidence of the status of income tax liability

4. To furnish assurance that a dispute with the Internal Revenue Service is disposed of conclusively

5. To determine cost or fair market value at a particular date.

Even if a closing agreement has been signed, there may be additional inspection of a taxpayer's records in order to determine whether fraud or misrepresentation of a material fact existed.

Refund Claims

A refund claim for federal income taxes must be filed within three years from the time the tax return was filed or two years from the time the tax was paid, whichever is later. Even though the Internal Revenue Service is barred from assessing additional tax because of the running of the regular three-year statute of limitations, the Service can re-audit the original tax return in order to determine if the amount claimed as a refund can be offset by an improper deduction or anything else which may be unearthed.

If a person files a federal income tax refund claim, he is permitted to sue the government for the money within two years from the date when the claim is rejected. When is that? Most people would think that this means the date on that notice of rejection of this claim. What it really means, a court decided in 1980, is the date on which the notice was *mailed*. And sometimes the problem is complicated by the fact that there is no postmark date on the envelope containing the rejection.

A refund claim must be filed with the I.R.S. before suit for recovery can be filed in court. Suit is permissible only after the claim is rejected or if no action is taken on it by the Service within six months.

7.
The Tyranny of Time

The federal income tax is based upon a person's income during his taxable year. As one court stated in one decision, "the annual accounting concept . . . is necessary for administration of the tax laws." For that reason, a party should seek to get items of income or deduction in whatever taxable year will benefit him the most. The element of timing can be as important to a taxpayer as it is to an athlete or to a comedian.

But although a person does have some choice as to the year in which he will earn income, such as by making a sale, or when he will take a deduction, such as by making a contribution, in most instances he is a prisoner of time. That is especially the situation in his dealings with the Internal Revenue Service. The tax law or the Treasury Department regulations impose a rigid timetable upon the taxpayer. But the Internal Revenue Service also is held to the same dates.

Filing Date

An individual must file his federal income tax return by the fifteenth day of the fourth month following the close of his taxable year. Although when a taxpayer is on the calendar year basis, this means the filing date is April 15, or the next business day if the fifteenth is a Sunday or holiday, not every individual uses a calendar year as his period of accounting. A fiscal year means a twelve-month period ending on the last day of any month except December. Although most individuals follow the calendar year, a person is free to elect another twelve-month period. For example, an individual who derives a substantial portion of his income from a partnership may wish to use the same period which the partnership employs, and that, for business reasons may end on August 31. Then the individual's federal income tax return is due on December 15.

You are in a rush to make a plane and don't want to waste time with last-minute mailings. Waste it anyway. A tax return, court petition for a hearing, election, and the like must be filed by specified dates. If your material arrives after that date, it still is deemed to have been received on time if the postmark on the envelope is no later than the last permissible date for filing. But that means a *United States* postmark. A document was held to be too late in a 1980 decision when the envelope arrived after the due date but had been mailed before that date in Canada.

The federal income tax return of a person who dies is due on the same date which would have been used had he not died.

Proof of mailing by the due date is not compliance with the requirement of mailing on time if full postage has not been prepaid. Nor is proof of delivery of the envelope to a professional courier service to assure speedy transmission acceptable if the material reaches the addressee one day late.

One 1980 case involved a person whose tax returns for several years never showed up on I.R.S. records, although he insisted that he had filed them all on time. Long after the event, he could not say for sure just when and where he had filed these returns. Under hypnosis by a professional technician, he later testified in court that he now could remember specifically the dates and places of mailing his returns for the past three years. That didn't persuade the court that the returns actually had been filed on time—if at all. No impartial person had been present to say whether the hypnotist had planted "suggestions" in his questions. And, as the I.R.S. suggested, the taxpayer may have "lived a lie so long that he no longer knew what the truth was."

Under most circumstances, husband and wife may submit a joint federal income tax return, which usually results in a lower total tax. The election to file a joint return may be made or changed until the expiration of the statute of limitations, which generally means three years. The election can't be made after the I.R.S. has mailed to either spouse a deficiency notice, if he or she seeks a Tax Court review of the amount allegedly owed. For this purpose, it doesn't matter whether the election to switch to a joint return is made before or after the request for tax court review is filed, says a 1980 decision.

If a federal income tax return lacks sufficient information for the proper computation of tax, it is not regarded as a tax return at all. So prosecution for failure to file a return is permitted.

Extension of Filing Date

If an individual is not able to get his income tax return filed by the last permissible date for filing, an extension of time to file the return should be obtained from the District Director of Internal Revenue for the place where he files his return, which usually is the place where he lives. This must be applied for *before* the due date of the tax return. Usually, an individual can in effect grant himself an extension of time for filing by sending in Form 4848, "Application for Automatic Extension of Time to File U.S. Individual Income Tax Return." Until recently, this had to be prepared in triplicate, the copies being used for (1) the application itself, (2) attachment to the income tax return when subsequently it is filed, and (3) the taxpayer's files. But although only one copy now must be submitted with the application, some persons still are submitting two copies with the thought that if one copy goes astray, there still will be on file a record that the application had been submitted before the due date of the tax return.

Estimated tax for the year must be shown on this form, or the request for extension will be denied. "Zero" or "None" may be shown as the estimated amount of tax, but such entries as "Unknown" or "Impossible to compute" will be rejected. No approval or acknowledgement will be sent by the Internal Revenue Service. The taxpayer will be notified only if his application is denied; otherwise, he has been granted two months additional for filing. Note that this extension covers only the filing date of the income tax form, not the time for the payment of tax.

An extension beyond this two-month period will be granted only for substantial reasons, which must be justified individually by reason of specifics involving the return in question. For this purpose, an individual should write a letter to the I.R.S. or, preferably, file Form 2688, "Application for Extension of Time to File U.S. Individual Income Tax Return." Only in exceptional situations will the Service accept this application unless Form 4848 previously had been filed on time. Form 2688 should be used in the case of such occurrences as destruction by fire or other casualty of the taxpayer's records. Acceptable as a hardship case for this purpose is the death or serious illness of the taxpayer, a member of his immediate family, his tax advisor, or a key member of the advisor's staff. Another acceptable reason is a civil disturbance. The nature of the alleged hardship should be noted on the application form. Two copies of the application must be sent to the Internal Revenue Service, one of the copies being for return to the taxpayer. The application must be completely self-explanatory, without reference to any earlier applications of correspondence. Any additional time for filing is requested by the submission of a *new* Form 2688, showing the *current* reason for the additional extension request.

An extension of more than six months' time will not be granted, unless the taxpayer is outside the United States.

Military personnel on duty outside of the United States or Puerto Rico are allowed an automatic two-month extension of time to file, as are United States citizens who are not in the United States or Puerto Rico on the filing date.

Requests for reconsideration of previously denied requests should be sent to the appropriate Internal Revenue Service center, not to the District office where tax returns are sent.

Payment of Tax

Any income tax shown on the tax return or the application for extension must be paid in full by filing date of the tax return, to the extent not already paid in the form of declarations of estimated tax, withholding by employers, or credits from prior years. If the I.R.S. computes an individual's tax, he will be sent a bill for any amount owing, payable within thirty days.

Payment may be made in the form of cash, checks, money orders, or U.S. Treasury bills, tax anticipation series. In certain circumstances, foreign currency will be accepted. But payment may not be made by credit card.

A District Director is authorized to refuse to accept any personal check if he has good reason (unspecified) to believe that this check will not be honored. A person who tenders a worthless check or money order in payment of taxes is subject to a penalty of 1% of the amount of the check, with a minimum $5 fine. But it is difficult to think of a less likely party to whom to give a bad check than the Internal Revenue Service.

It is inadvisable to make out a check for federal taxes to "IRS." If such a remittance is lost or stolen, these letters easily can be converted to "MRS," with an appropriate name then being added.

Upon request, the Service will issue a receipt for tax payments.

Late Filing

Penalties for late filing may be imposed by the Internal Revenue Service. See Chapter 8, "Fines And Penalties. Interest."

Other unpleasant things result from failure to file a federal income tax return on time. The statute of limitations begins with the filing of the tax return, and an unfiled return extends the time in which the I.R.S. may make an audit, perhaps into perpetuity. Certain elections are available to a taxpayer when it seems advantageous to him; but unless this election is made on a tax return which is filed on time, the election does not count. Examples are the reporting of certain sales on the installment plan or the deferring of gain on an involuntary conversion, such as where a home is destroyed by fire and the insurance company's settlement check is more than the cost or adjusted basis of the property.

Proof of Timely Filing

It is a taxpayer's responsibility to be able to *prove* that his tax return was filed on time if he would avoid interest, penalty, and other consequences of tardy or omitted filing. Posting a tax return to the Internal Revenue Service is not enough: can you definitely establish when this took place? Ordinarily a postmark by the United States Postal Service will show that filing was not later than the required due date, but envelopes deposited in a mail box may not be postmarked by the post office until the next day, and that one day means the difference between filing on time and not doing so. The date on metered mail establishes nothing as to the date of filing, because a person could control the date on his own machine, even if in fact he did not do so.

A popular but dangerous fallacy is that if you mail a tax document before the due date, it is deemed to have been filed on time, even if it arrives belatedly. But that is true only if it actually arrives, so that proof of timely mailing can be established by the postmark. One communication was mailed by a taxpayer's attorney ahead of time. It never arrived. The taxpayer vainly argued that he should not be penalized because of a failure by the U.S. Postal Service. You could have avoided that situation, advised the court in a 1981 decision, had you sent the communication by registered mail, where the date of registration is deemed to be the postmark.

Even registered mail, return receipt requested, does not establish that a tax return, refund claim, or any other document was sent to the Internal Revenue Service on time, for all that this receipt proves is that *something* was sent to the Service on time, the exact nature of which is left to the taxpayer to prove. In one case, the taxpayer's production of a registered mail receipt was of no help to him, because the I.R.S. showed the court that it had received a letter from him on the same day, referring to an entirely different matter. The taxpayer lost because he was not able to show that something other than this irrelevant letter also had been in the same envelope, which indeed might have been the case.

One of the worst conflagrations in the modern history of the New York City Fire Department involved a mid-city post office. It is obvious that a taxpayer could not meet his burden of timely submission of tax documents when envelopes as well as contents have been destroyed.

Notify the I.R.S. When You Move

A person will lose by default if he does not file a protest to, or appeal from, an unfavorable tax action within the time specified for this, such as the thirty days permitted for a review in most instances. If he fails to pay a deficiency notice on time, there can be consequences ranging from imposition of interest to seizure of his property for nonpayment of taxes. The Internal Revenue Service has met its obligation if it mails correspondence, inquiries, notifications, and demands to a taxpayer at his last known address. When a person moves, it may take more time for official correspondence to catch up with him than he has within which to act without forfeiting rights or incurring penalties. So when there is a change of address, notify not only your friends and business associates and magazines to which you subscribe, but also the Postal Service. And make certain to advise the Internal Revenue Service of any change in that last known address, which otherwise will be used. Equally important, be prepared to prove that you sent your new address to the I.R.S.

One case involved an individual whose mailbox outside of his home had been ransacked by vandals. But he continued to show his home address on his federal income tax return, although he had notified the Postal Service to send mail to his office rather than to the ravaged home mailbox. A deficiency notice was sent by the I.R.S. to his home, the communication being returned to the sender by the Postal Service with the notation that the box had been discontinued. When this demand for tax finally reached the taxpayer, it was too late for him to apply to the Tax Court for a review of the matter. That the notice caught up with him belatedly was adjudged to be his own fault.

As the court stated in one decision, ''it is the taxpayer who has the duty to keep the Commissioner [of Internal Revenue] informed with an up-to-date address.''

A person can appoint an attorney to represent him before the I.R.S. in connection with the examination of his federal income tax return. The Service's rules of procedure state that a copy of any communication to a

113

taxpayer will be given to his recognized representative, if his authority is on file. This can prevent non-response to a tax inquiry while a taxpayer is away on business or otherwise.

Jeopardy Assessment

Federal income tax is fully payable by the prescribed filing date for the return. But when the Internal Revenue Service believes collection would be endangered if tax is not paid upon a person's income earned period to the time a tax return is due, a District Director can issue a *jeopardy assessment,* which calls for tax payments at this time instead of when the tax return normally would be due and tax would be payable. For example, the I.R.S. may have reason to suspect that a taxpayer is disposing of or concealing assets, or that he is getting ready to go underground. A jeopardy assessment is issued in order to collect taxes while payment still can be enforced. A court will grant an injunction against such an assessment only where (1) the taxpayer can show that under no circumstances could the Service win its case if the matter were litigated *and* (2) irreparable injury would result if the injunction were not granted. Certain taxpayers have been unable to get a court to enjoin a jeopardy assessment, despite their plea that such an assessment "stripped them of their assets and [they] are unable to defend themselves against an onslaught of litigation by the United States involving [huge sums of money] and consequently face complete financial ruin." The injunction was denied, because the taxpayers could not show that the government was certain to lose in court.

Customarily, the I.R.S. uses this procedure only when there is reason to believe that a taxpayer is concealing assets or is about to slip out of the country. But in addition to these sinister implications, a jeopardy assessment also can be imposed where, in the words of the Treasury regulations, "The taxpayer's financial solvency is or appears to be imperiled."

After a jeopardy assessment has been made, the I.R.S. must send the taxpayer a statement which shows the basis for the assessment. The taxpayer has thirty days from this point, or thirty-five days from the printed assessment notice date should that be earlier, in which to apply for a review by the District Director.

When the review has been made, the taxpayer has thirty days (sixteen days from the request for a review, if that comes first) in which to start litigation in the District Court for a judicial review. Here, the Service must prove that the jeopardy assessment is reasonable, and the court must issue its ruling within twenty days. The taxpayer may ask for an extension of not more than forty days, as where it takes time to assemble relevant data. The opinion itself is not subject to appeal.

Termination of Taxable Year

If the Internal Revenue Service believes that tax collection would be imperilled by waiting until a person's taxable year ends, that year may be terminated by the Service at once so that tax can be assessed and collected. In one situation when this happened, the I.R.S. wrote to the taxpayer that a court would review the correctness of this termination order if suit were filed by May 9. The letter should have said May 2. But when suit was filed by the taxpayer on May 9, it was rejected by the court as too late. Inasmuch as the time provided by law expired on May 2, there was nothing the Service or the court could do about the mistaken date, even though the I.R.S. had made the error—in writing. The only protection against this sort of thing is for a taxpayer to check all applicable dates, regardless of what he has been told by the appropriate government employee.

The I.R.S. has to establish that its action in not awaiting the close of the regular taxable year was reasonable under the circumstances. When Revenue Agents questioned one person about a recent large deposit and its prompt withdrawal, he burst out that he never again would leave any assets within reach of the government. To the court that justified the Service belief that he was going to skip the country, and the termination assessment was permitted. Subsequent suggestions that the money came from the sale of his home, which might have qualified for long-term or deferral treatment for tax purposes, did not mean that the Service had acted unreasonably in light of what had seemed like suspicious behavior at that time, especially what he had exclaimed in his anger.

Appeals of Tax Rulings and Decisions

The times within which appeals can be made to higher authority within the Internal Revenue Service, or to the courts, have been discussed in Chapter 6, "When You and the Revenue Agent Can't Agree."

Refund Claims

After a federal income tax return has been filed, a claim for refund may be filed within three years from the date the return was filed. Returns filed before the due date are considered to have been filed on the due date for this purpose. Alternatively, the refund claim may be filed within two years from the date the tax was paid, if that is a later date. One refund claim was filed after the permissible date, with the explanation that all facts necessary for the determination of correct tax liability had not been known previously. That was immaterial. The time for filing the claim was set by law. It could not be changed by the Internal Revenue Service or the court for any reason.

If you don't file a proper tax return, you can forfeit a valid tax refund. One person filed her tax return form so incompletely filled in that it was characterized as "no return." She was not permitted to file her claim up to three years from the filing date of the return, for "no return" had been filed and hence there was no filing date.

The refund claim of an individual formerly was filed on a special refund claim form. Now the I.R.S. requires the filing of an amended income tax return, showing the item corrected as it *should* be. Used for this purpose is Form 1040X, "Amended U.S. Individual Income Tax Return." A separate Form 1040X must be filed for each taxable year involved. A statement is attached to this, which backs up the claim with an explanation of each item of income, deduction, or credit at issue.

If the refund claim is filed within three years of the date when the tax return was filed, the credit or refund may not exceed the portion of the tax paid within a period, immediately preceding the filing of the claim, equal to three years plus any extension of time for filing the return. If the claim is not filed within this three-year period, the credit or refund may not exceed the portion of the tax paid during the two years immediately preceding the filing of the claim.

Special rules exist for later filing of refund claims which are based on a bad debt, worthless security, net operating loss carryback, capital loss carryback, or foreign tax credit. In addition, longer time is available for filing a refund claim where the taxpayer and the I.R.S. previously had entered into an agreement to extend the period of time, such as where some controversial point had to be straightened out and more time was required so that hasty action would not be taken.

Involuntary Conversion of Property

If property is destroyed by casualty, or if it is condemned by a governmental authority for public use, there is an *involuntary conversion*. Should the owner receive more from an insurance company or governmental agency than the tax cost of the property in his hands, he has taxable gain. But it may be possible to elect to postpone paying federal income tax on all or part of this gain.

No gain is recognized for tax purposes to the extent that what the owner receives is reinvested in property of the like kind to that destroyed or condemned. The replacement period for real property held for productive use in a trade or business or for investment ends three years after the close of the first taxable year in which any part of the gain upon the conversion is realized. The replacement period for all other property ends two years after the close of the first taxable year in which any gain is realized.

If a person sells his principal residence at a profit, he has no taxable gain to the extent that he re-invests the proceeds in a new principal residence and occupies it within eighteen months. If he can't meet this condition, irrespective of why, gain is taxed. A construction strike, a fire, a financing problem, or inability to find just what was desired can result in taxability.

An extension of the replacement period may be granted if an application is made to the Internal Revenue Service. This is sent to the same place as the tax return on which the election to postpone tax on the gain was filed. The election itself is made on the tax return for the taxable year in which gain was realized.

When Is a Tax Matter Closed?

A case *agreed to* at the District Director level is considered to be closed when the taxpayer is notified in writing of any changes which are acceptable to both parties, or that no changes are to be made.

An *unagreed* tax case is considered to be closed when the period for filing a petition for review with the United States Tax Court expires, if no petition was filed.

The Internal Revenue Service will not reopen any case closed by a District office to make an adjustment unfavorable to the taxpayer unless:

1. There is evidence of fraud, wrongdoing, collusion, concealment or misrepresentation of a material fact; or

2. The prior closing involved a clearly defined substantial error based upon an established I.R.S. position existing at the time of the previous examination; or

3. Other circumstances exist which indicate failure to reopen would be a serious administrative omission.

The issuance of a refund check to a taxpayer does not necessarily mean that the matter is closed. One individual filed an income tax refund claim on Form 1040X. The Internal Revenue Service asked for further information about a car said to have been used for business purposes. While this was being considered, other Service personnel (or machines) sent him a refund check. Highly elated that justice had triumphed, he threw out such records as he had on the car depreciation matter, believing that his receipt of the check signalled the ending of any controversy. But it did not. As he no longer was in position to document the deduction, it was not allowed.

Recovery of Seized Property

One of the Internal Revenue Service's alternatives when there are unpaid taxes is to seize and to sell a taxpayer's property. The owner of real estate thus seized can redeem the property within 120 days after the sale by paying the buyer the purchase price plus interest at the rate of 20% per annum. One taxpayer sought to do this, but the permissible 120th day coincided with the Great Blizzard of 1978 in Massachusetts, and the county where the buyer lived was shut down for a week by the state governor. The day that this ban was lifted, the taxpayer sought to redeem his property. It was too late. The time for redemption under the tax laws cannot be extended even by a court. Nor could the closing of the roads to non-essential travel by the governor be equated with state holidays, which automatically extend tax law dates to the next business day. "Legal holiday" means a state-wide legal holiday and here only certain counties were involved. The court was not exactly sympathetic to this frustrated taxpayer, declaring: "Having waited so long, and taken the risk of unforeseen consequences of their own delay, they should not now be heard to complain of the Great Blizzard."

Real estate seized by the Internal Revenue Service for back taxes similarly can be redeemed from the Service within 120 days by paying these taxes in full. But if the payment on that 120th day proves to be too low, there is no time to straighten out the matter. That was learned by a taxpayer, who paid the Service a tax which according to his records was $52,906.07. But his computation was too low by $30.57, and he did not get his property back.

Request for a Prompt Assessment

As has been noted previously, the Internal Revenue Service ordinarily must make an audit within three years of the due date of an income tax return. But when a taxpayer has died, the executor of his estate can make a request for a prompt assessment, which has to be performed within eighteen months.

Voluntary Disclosure of Wrongdoing

A person can file an amended federal income tax return until the statute of limitations expires. After that time, even if he has a change of heart, he cannot escape the consequences of fraud, that is, willful evasion of taxes known to be due, by making a voluntary disclosure of his misdeeds. That is the case even though the Internal Revenue Service has not yet discovered them and perhaps never would.

I.R.S. Is Also Bound by the Handcuffs of Time

The Internal Revenue Service must adhere to the rules of time, such as the statute of limitations, in the same manner that a taxpayer is obliged to do. For example, if the Service issues a tax deficiency notice one day after the time limit for notification, it is too late. The taxpayer is not obligated to pay it. The matter is closed. In one case, the I.R.S. sent a deficiency notice to a person who lived in Honduras. This was sent by certified mail, which can be used only for domestic deliveries, and the Postal Service returned the envelope to the sender. It was at once sent out again by registered mail, but now the postmark was one day too late to be effective.

The I.R.S. erroneously sent a refund check to an individual. Five years later, the Service sued him for recovery of this amount. The court rejected the suit because the government had to start suit for an erroneous refund within two years of its having been paid. (The time is five years if the refund had been obtained through misrepresentation, which hadn't been the case here.) The court said it was "reluctant to place a premium on a clerical mistake," but the taxpayer could keep that erroneous refund we all dream about.

Taxpayers should check deficiency notices, requests to make an additional examination, and other I.R.S. communications very carefully. The tyranny of time can hobble the Service as well as the taxpayer.

8.
Fines and Penalties. Interest

The purpose of imposing fines and penalties upon persons who attempt to defraud the revenue, declared the United States Supreme Court, is to enforce the collection of taxes. These penalties are intended to instill fear "upon parties whose conscientious scruples are not sufficient to balance their hope of profit." Lesser fines and penalties may be imposed upon other parties whose tax shortcomings were ignorance or carelessness rather than hope of profit. One of the rewards for being a good taxpayer is the saving of fines, penalties, and interest. This reward can be quite substantial, considering the alternatives.

Federal income tax fines and penalties may be of either of two types. There are *ad valorem* penalties, with a specified percentage being applied to the tax. And there are specific dollar fines, or years of imprisonment, without reference to the amount of tax which triggered this action.

Ad Valorem Penalties

The principal *ad valorem* penalties are:

- 5% of the tax in the case of negligence, such as carelessness, ignorance, or an honest mistake.
- 50% of the tax in case of fraud, which is willful evasion of taxes known to be due.
- One-half of 1% per month, with a maximum of 25%, of delinquency in making payments.
- 5% of the tax for failure to file a tax return on time, plus an additional 5% per month or fraction thereof, the total not to exceed 25%.

Late filing of an income tax return can involve two penalties: (1) failure to file on time, and (2) failure to make timely payment of tax which must accompany the return. Under each of (1) and (2), the tax law states that the addition to tax for tardiness is to be increased for each month of delay, "not exceeding 25 percent in the aggregate." One person received from the I.R.S. an "Explanation of Penalty or Interest Charges," which said that "the combined penalty is not more than 25 percent of the tax not timely paid." When the actual bill came in, however, this limitation was placed on (1) and also on (2) separately, with the result that the total assessed came to more than 25% despite what the Service explanation had stated. But the taxpayer had to pay the full amount billed. An I.R.S. explanation is no authority when a court interprets the law.

One individual employed an accountant to prepare his federal income tax return. The return was filed belatedly because, said the accountant, there were unexpected complications. The late filing charge was imposed upon the taxpayer, for the accountant was merely his agent.

A taxpayer worked as an accountant for the Armed Forces. He was hurt in an accident on April 14, suffering a leg injury which caused him to be sent to a hospital, where he remained for a week. Meanwhile, the tax return wasn't filed by April 15. He argued that no penalty should be imposed because the late filing was due to reasonable cause: he was in pain. But the court found that he had no reasonable cause for failure to file his tax return on time, for he could have guided his wife, a book-keeper, as to what to do.

An individual may be exposed to penalty for certain shortcomings of a specialized nature. For example, a person who is not covered by his employer's qualified pension plan may set up his own Individual Retirement Account (IRA) plan, to which he can contribute and deduct up to 15% of his year's compensation, but not more than $1,500. But there is a 6% excise tax on any higher amount he puts into the account, unless he takes it out again by the time he files his federal income tax return. More detailed reference to this will be made later in the chapter.

Specific Penalties

Any person required to collect, account for, and pay over any tax who willfully fails to do so is—in addition to any other penalties provided by law—guilty of a felony and upon conviction is subject to a fine of not more than $10,000, or imprisonment for not more than five years, or both. In addition, as a crowning indignity, he has to pay for the cost of his own prosecution.

There is a fine of not more than $5,000, or imprisonment for not more than three years, or both, together with the costs of prosecution, if a person: (1) declares under penalty of perjury anything which he does not believe to be true and correct as to every material matter; (2) willfully aids or assists in the preparation or filing of a return, affidavit, claim, or other document covered by the internal revenue laws, if the item is fraudulent or false as to any material matter; (3) removes or conceals with intent to defraud any goods or commodities or other property upon which a tax levy is authorized; or (4) conceals property or withholds, falsifies, or destroys records in connection with a compromise or closing agreement with the Internal Revenue Service.

If there is a willful disclosure or delivery to the Internal Revenue Service of any list, return, account, statement, or other document, known to the person supplying these data to be false as to any material account, there is a fine of not more than $1,000, imprisonment of not more than one year, or both.

Where anyone corruptly or by force or threat of force endeavors to intimidate any officer or employee of the United States in the administration of the tax law, there is a fine of not more than $5,000 or imprisonment of not more than three years, or both. But if the offense is committed only by threats of force, the cost drops to not more than $3,000 or one year, or both. This includes any threatening letter or communication.

Kicking about a Revenue Agent shouldn't be with one's feet. An eighty-four-year-old attorney was accused of the crime of assaulting a Revenue Agent during the course of a tax examination. But in his own defense, the octogenerian taxpayer claimed that if he had been guilty of anything, it was that, in his own words, he didn't "kick him harder and quicker and longer." Price for this form of self-expression: $3,000.

If a person forcibly recues property after it has been seized by the Internal Revenue Service for nonpayment of taxes, or causes the property thus to be rescued by other parties, there is a fine of $500, or not more than double the value of the property, whichever is greater, or imprisonment for not more than two years. Even if the I.R.S. seizes a taxpayer's property without a court order, the property cannot be seized back. One individual who did this was fined for interfering with the administration of the tax laws.

Anyone who enters into an agreement or conspiracy to defraud the United States, or any of its departments or agencies, by obtaining or helping to obtain the payment or allowance of any false, fictitious, or fraudulent claim can be fined not more than $1,000 or imprisoned not more than ten years, or both.

Any person who ignores a summons, or an order to appear and produce books, accounts, records, memoranda, or any other papers is subject to a fine of not more than $1,000 or imprisonment of not more than one year, or both.

Any individual required to supply information to his employer for withholding tax purposes who willfully supplies false or fraudulent information, or no information at all, is subject to a fine of not more than $500, or imprisonment for not more than one year, or both. The reason for supplying false information to one's employer is immaterial. For example, a single woman would be subject to these penalties if she falsely reported on Form W–4, "Employee's Withholding Exemption Certificate," that she was married. Her statement actually might have been made in an apparently justifiable attempt to discourage the office wolves.

An employer required to furnish an employee a statement of amounts withheld from his compensation, who willfully supplies a false or fraudulent statement, or none at all, is punishable by a fine of not more than $1,000, or imprisonment for not more than one year, or both.

The Pension Reform Act of 1974 imposes a variety of penalties for cases in which employees covered by a plan are not provided with required information. Willfully supplying a false or fraudulent statement to an employee costs $50 for each act or failure. A pension plan administrator who fails to file the actuarial report called for by law may have to pay a penalty of $1,000 for each such failure. There are various penalties for violation of fiduciary obligations in the case of a pension plan.

Failure to inform recipients of interest, dividends, and certain other forms of income is subject to a fine of $10 a return, not to exceed $25,000 for all payees in that year.

Starting in 1979, a penalty is imposed upon partnerships for failure to file an income tax return on time. This penalty is in addition to the regular criminal penalties for willful failure to file a return, to supply information, or to pay a tax. This penalty is assessed for each month or fraction thereof (not to exceed five) that the partnership return is late or incomplete. The penalty for each month or fraction is $50 multiplied by the total number of partners in the partnership that year. But penalty will not be imposed if the partnership can show that the failure to file a timely or complete return is due to reasonable cause.

A businessperson may feel honored if he or she is asked to serve as an official of a worthy charitable foundation. But it can cost this person dearly. A foundation is required by law to publish a notice that its annual report is available for public inspection. This is so that anyone can determine whether a contribution to the foundation will get him an income tax deduction. But that makes the notice an essential type of tax return. In one case, an individual whose general responsibilities covered such things as the publication of the notice was fined $5,000 because the announcement had not been made. It was irrelevant that he had relied upon professional advisors to tell him what had to be done. The court noted that "the filing of a tax return is a personal non-delegable duty on the part of the taxpayer."

If anyone brings a matter to the United States Tax Court merely to delay the collection of taxes, and that matter is suspended until that tribunal renders an opinion which becomes final, there can be a fine not in excess of $500.

There is a penalty of $10 a day, up to a maximum of $5,000, for failure to file Form 5239, "Return for Individual Retirement Savings Arrangement." This form must be filed with an individual's federal income tax return. A person is not permitted to maintain an IRA if he or she is covered by an employer's pension plan. One self-employed person properly maintained an IRA with an insurance company, to which she made payments up to the amount which is permitted as a tax deduction. When she obtained a position with a corporation which included her in its pension plan, she asked Internal Revenue Service representatives whether she should continue contributing to her own IRA. She was advised "to hold on to it." That was wrong advice. Her deduction for payments to the insurance company was disallowed. She was also penalized for making an excess contribution, the entire payment being deemed "excess" because she should not have been continuing the account after she became covered by her employer's pension plan. The court noted, sadly, that "unfair as it sometimes may appear to taxpayers, erroneous legal advice is not binding on the Commissioner of Internal Revenue." She incurred penalty as a result of relying upon this advice.

One employee worked for a corporation which had a pension plan, which did not include him because he had not worked for a sufficiently long period to qualify. So he made contributions to an IRA which he set up. On the last day of the taxable year, the corporation changed its policy about which employees should be covered, and the plan was amended to cover him retroactively for that year. Being covered by an employer's pension plan that year because of this change of mind, his contributions to the IRA were disallowed, and he had to pay a penalty because of the excess amount of his contribution, that is, the entire amount paid during the year.

Another form of penalty is brought to an individual's attention in the words which are printed directly over the line which he must sign on his federal income tax return: "Under penalties of perjury, I declare that I have examined this return, including accompanying schedules and statements, and to the best of my knowledge and belief, it is true, correct, and complete."

If a taxpayer pays his taxes with a check which is not honored by his bank, here is what the Internal Revenue Service will penalize him for that caper:

- For a check of $5 or more, $5 or 1% of the total, whichever is less.
- For a check of $2 to $4.99, the amount of the check.
- For a check of less than $2, nothing will happen.

Negligence or Fraud

When federal income tax has been underpaid, it is important to establish whether this was because of negligence or fraud. As mentioned earlier in this chapter, the penalty is 5% in the case of the former and 50% in the case of the latter. But fraud has serious consequences other than the 50% penalty. There can be dollar fines and/or prison terms. The statute of limitations never ends, which means that the Internal Revenue Service can audit the tax return and assess additional tax regardless of how many years have elapsed since the filing date. The fraud penalty is imposed not only upon the fraudulent understatement of taxable income. If there is fraud, the 50% applies to the entire amount of underpaid tax, even items which represented innocent and honest errors.

A taxpayer has to prove that he was not negligent in order to avoid penalty. But the Internal Revenue Service has to prove the existence of fraud, the willful attempt to evade taxes known to be due.

A negligence penalty may be imposed even where the negligence was not willful, as where a person just forgot to sign his tax return. If someone takes a deduction on his tax return without bothering to find out whether the item really is deductible, should he be in error, the resultant tax can be swollen with a negligence penalty, because reasonable care had not been taken to reflect taxable income correctly. When an individual made a gift of wine that he found in the cellar of his new home, he was penalized for negligence in not filing a gift tax return. He did not know that the value of this wine was high enough to require the filing of a gift tax return, but he was negligent in having failed to check the matter of value with a wine expert.

What you don't pay a tax advisor you may have to pay instead to the

I.R.S. One person sought to reduce taxes by setting up a "family trust." The many technical requirements were not all met, and he had to pay additional tax on his income which allegedly had been channelled to the trust. In addition, he was penalized for negligence because he had tried to handle everything himself without mastering the law's complexities. "We think," declared a 1980 decision, "a step so drastic as [assignment of income to a trust] was one in which a reasonable, prudent person would have consulted a competent tax advisor."

An individual's tax return showed a capital loss on the sale of stock. Although he sold stock on thirteen different occasions that year, only one sale was reported. Various deductions he claimed improperly were disallowed by the I.R.S., and to the tax deficiency resulting from these was added a negligence penalty for intentional disregard of the rules and regulations, that is, failing to report all of his stock losses. The fact that he would have reported a larger capital loss than he could have utilized, had he shown all of his stock transactions, did not excuse him from his duty to report them, according to a 1980 decision.

But courts have held that negligence was not involved where a taxpayer made a mistake which involved the interpretation of a highly complex provision in the law. No one should be penalized, stated one court, for inability to figure out the proper tax consequences of an extremely complicated happening, even though he may have had considerable experience in tax matters.

Failure to maintain adequate records for the determination of taxable income is regarded as negligence.

Even if a taxpayer has been guilty of negligence, penalty may be waived if he can show that what he did or failed to do resulted from *reasonable cause*. Examples of this are illness at the time the tax return was being filed, destruction of records by fire or other causes beyond the taxpayer's control, continuing to treat deductions in the same manner as in prior years which had been examined by Revenue Agents without objection or question. Penalty also may be waived if a person can show that he relied upon the advice of a competent advisor to whom a full disclosure of all of the facts were made.

In most situations, a taxpayer can avoid negligence penalty for omitting income or taking an improper deduction if he is able to show that (1) he had *relied* upon the advice of (2) a *competent* person to whom (3) a *full disclosure* of all of the facts had been made. The tough part is (1), since a professional person whose expertise is on the line may be inclined to deny having given the wrong advice. In one case, a misadvised taxpayer avoided penalty when additional tax was assessed because of his forethought in having gotten a lawyer to put his (flawed) opinion on paper. This established that the error was not because of the taxpayer's negligence. And if pressed to put his opinion in writing, an advisor probably will consider it more carefully.

One person, perplexed as to whether certain receipts were taxable, questioned his attorney, a thoroughly experienced tax lawyer and teacher. The attorney and a C.P.A. asked an I.R.S. agent, showing him the text of a recent court decision involving another party, which had held that similar receipts were not taxable. The agent suggested that the taxpayer write on his return that no tax was due on the basis of a court decision, a copy of which was attached to the return. Subsequently this decision was reversed by a higher court. Based upon this, a Revenue Agent imposed tax on the transaction. That was proper. But penalty could not be imposed, for the taxpayer had a reasonable cause for failing to report the questioned item as income.

If experts can't agree as to the meaning of a highly complex provision of the law, a taxpayer cannot be penalized for fraud where he has failed to show a transaction under this provision is not taxable.

Being "too busy" is not an acceptable excuse for omitting income from a tax return or for filing belatedly. In the words of one court, "A plea of 'too busy' is insufficient to relieve the taxpayer or his legal representative of the obligation imposed by the statute to make timely filing."

Fraud involves intentional wrongdoing on the part of the taxpayer for the purpose of evading a tax known or believed to be owing. Inasmuch as the Internal Revenue Service rarely can prove what a taxpayer actually knew or believed, the I.R.S. customarily wins a fraud case by showing that tax understatement could have resulted only from deliberate attempt to evade taxes.

Here are examples of what the courts concluded were willful attempts to evade taxes. One individual reported much lower income on his tax return than he showed on a sworn statement submitted to his bank when he applied for a loan. In other cases, assets were concealed, or were recorded in someone else's name. Essential records were destroyed at about the same time as the I.R.S. showed an interest in seeing them. False entries were made in the books. Records customarily kept in transactions of a certain type were not maintained. Cash receipts were insisted upon even when a customer, patient, or client wanted to pay by check. A taxpayer failed to supply data requested by his tax return preparer and concealed pertinent information from her. A person failed to tell his own accountant of the existence of certain sources of income. False statements were made to a Revenue Agent. Two sets of books were maintained.

There is a fine of up to $500, or a year in prison, or both, for willfully filing a false withholding exemption certificate with your employer. It doesn't matter, says a 1980 decision, that you had no evil intent, such as avoiding federal taxes. So if a person feels that in poor economic times his employer is less likely to drop someone with six children than only one, he may be tempted to list six children. His child may not see him again for a year.

Perhaps you are genuinely busy. Perhaps you regard the questions as irrelevant or even impertinent. Perhaps you just don't like government agents or the personality of the particular individual. But failure to co-operate with a Revenue Agent can subject you to fraud penalty, that is, willfully concealing income with intent to avoid tax.

Rarely can the I.R.S. show, as it must to establish a fraud case, that a taxpayer *willfully* had attempted to conceal his known tax liability, for how can it be demonstrated what a person really had in mind? But circumstances can convict a taxpayer by suggesting that what he actually had been thinking about was concealing taxable income from the I.R.S. In a 1980 case, one person was found to have attempted to frustrate a thorough examination of his tax returns by permitting the Revenue Agent to examine the records only in an unheated back room.

If a person has had considerable experience in tax matters, or has had technical training in the field, a court is likely to conclude that any item improperly handled on the tax return could have resulted only from deliberate attempt to understate income. How could a party with such a background not have known better than to report income as he did?

Exact numbers on an income tax return may suggest that they had been fabricated. For example, the Service zeroed in on one return where income was shown as exactly $24,000 and itemized deductions were precisely $5,500.

If you are extremely successful in business, understatement of your federal income tax is likely to be regarded as deliberate fraud rather than negligence. How could a person with such financial ability understate his income unless he were deliberately trying to evade taxes? But a 1980 case shows how facts can indicate that income omission was a matter of simple innocent ignorance. A person with only a fifth grade education for years had had a low-volume business and was in a poor cash flow position. Owing in part to the government's insistence that minority groups receive a fair share of U.S. contracts, his business boomed dramatically. But he still continued his haphazard, informal financial ways, and he continued to employ the same accountant, whose skills were limited to small, simple businesses. He just didn't realize how well his business really was doing when his records failed to disclose all of his income, because, as so often happens with a rapidly growing business, new inventory and equipment demands created the poor cash flow position which he always had associated with low earnings.

Sometimes, at the end of a tax audit, the Internal Revenue Service gives a taxpayer an "inadequate records notice." No penalty is imposed; this is a warning. But if the Service finds that the records still are inadequate when examined in connection with an audit of a subsequent year, any tax deficiency can be subjected to a fraud penalty, for by now the taxpayer must have learned that certain back-up records or substantiation is required, yet he had done nothing about complying with what he now knows are the requirements.

A person may feel that it is necessary to make payments which he prefers not to be known to his spouse, business associates, or anybody else; so the items are paid and deducted under harmless designations. But if this is discovered by a Revenue Agent, there can be a fraud penalty even though the actual amount of taxable income is correctly shown. Without truthful representation as to all matters, it becomes difficult if not impossible for the Internal Revenue Service to verify the tax returns. So the government may properly prosecute a taxpayer for falsely classifying items on his tax return. The taxpayer's statement directly below the perjury declaration, referred to earlier in this chapter, refers to the tax return's entries to be "true, correct, and complete."

Because of the I.R.S.'s huge automatic data processing system and other investigative apparatus, taxpayers may shy away from taking liberties on their federal returns, leaving such tax-saving tactics to state and local returns. But the more mechanically sophisticated federal examiners may apprehend state tax cheaters. The mailing of a false state return, a 1980 decision held, is a violation of federal postal laws.

A person may be subjected to fraud penalty even if his own income tax return is not involved. If you help someone else to cheat on his taxes, you can be found guilty of fraud because of attempting "in any manner to evade or defeat any tax imposed by" the law. It is a felony for a person knowingly to assist another party in the preparation and filing of a false and fraudulent tax return, regardless of whether the person being "helped" knows what is going on.

Sometimes one takes a calculated risk on his federal income tax return. He may choose to overlook reporting income from some obscure source, feeling that (1) no one is apt to discover the item and (2) even if a Revenue Agent is unusually alert and unearths it, the extra tax cost of some minor fraudulent omissions cannot amount to much. But if there has been a single deliberate attempt to evade taxes known to be due, this is a fraudulent tax return, and all under-reported income will be subject to the 50% fraud penalty. The discovery of even a modest instance of fraud by a tax examiner can poison the entire atmosphere of an audit.

Protest of Penalties

Federal income tax penalties, even if the taxpayer regards them as unjustified, have to be paid. Then he may apply for a refund if, for example, he shows reasonable cause for the transgression. That can involve time and money, depending upon how far he is willing to go in order to get his payment back. In 1978, the Internal Revenue Service devised a new procedure. If a taxpayer asks the I.R.S. to cancel a penalty and predictably the request is turned down, he can appeal to an official known as the Collection Conferee, available in each of the Service's districts. The expectation is that this Conferee will be able to dispose of an appeal within thirty days. If his decision is unfavorable, the slow old refund route still may be utilized. This procedure offers most promise in areas where reasonable cause is justification for waiving a penalty. It is not available where a penalty is automatic, such as for failure to pay estimated income tax.

Deductibility of Fines and Penalties

Fines and penalties paid to the Internal Revenue Service are not deductible for tax purposes. Sometimes the argument is raised that that's not what the payment really was. Where a corporation failed to send the I.R.S. the payroll and withholding taxes deducted from employees' wages, the officer charged with the duty of transmitting these taxes to the Service was obliged by law to make these payments out of his own pocket. But he was not permitted to deduct the amounts as expenses in connection with his business of being a corporate officer. Whatever he might have called the payment, it was a fine, a penalty for violating his legal duty to see that the withheld taxes were turned over to the government.

Sometimes when a party is convicted of violating a law having nothing whatsoever to do with taxation, a court will permit the violator to "make it up to the community" by paying the fine in the form of contributions to deserving charitable organizations. Contributions to approved charitable organizations, within limits set by the tax law, are deductible. The question is whether these payments really are deductible contributions or non-deductible penalties. What is decisive is not the label but what the payment actually represents.

Although fines and penalties for violation of a law are not deductible, one taxpayer claimed that what Congress had in mind as nondeductible was any action that evidenced that "reprehensible conduct" which normally accompanies the violation of a criminal law. In this case, the violation was of a federal safety act, which the taxpayer had used due care in seeking to obey. It simply had not been possible for the taxpayer always to identify and to correct operating conditions which happened to violate the law. The taxpayer's violations had resulted from sheer inability to find every violation of the safety law, not because of criminal intent or reprehensible conduct. That didn't make any difference, held a 1980 decision. There had been penalties. They were not deductible.

What the I.R.S. Can Do to a Reluctant Taxpayer

If a person fails to cooperate with the Internal Revenue Service in the payment of taxes, the government has a choice of many ways of overcoming his defiance:

1. A taxpayer's property may be seized and impounded, which means that a person cannot use his own property. Actually, it no longer is his and can be sold to raise funds for the payment of taxes. The Service is concerned primarily with getting enough for the property to cover unpaid taxes, and efforts to sell assets for their real value may not be pursued too energetically. Whatever the I.R.S. gets for the property, customarily at an auction sale, in excess of the amount of taxes owed belongs to the taxpayer. But often there is the suspicion that all the government wants to get from the sale is money to pay the taxes, so the assets may be sold at too low a figure, for example, without trying to locate all possible buyers.

If a taxpayer sues the I.R.S. for the excess of what the property should have brought and what the Service received, a court will reject the claim because the government cannot be sued without its consent, which is not likely to be given in such a situation.

2. A sign may be posted on a taxpayer's property, informing the world that this is now the property of the United States by reason of nonpayment of taxes. This notification obviously will hurt the taxpayer's financial standing, credit rating, and reputation, and it is very effective in forcing him to dig up the necessary cash somehow, for example by tapping the funds set aside for the children's education.

Where the I.R.S. has padlocked a taxpayer's premises for nonpayment of taxes, this can result in a bank's refusal to extend credit because of doubt as to ability to repay if the plant is shut down. In one case where this was exactly what happened, the taxpayer vainly sought to have the Service free the plant for a return to production in return for a promise to pay off these taxes according to an installment schedule. The court declined to order the I.R.S. to release the factory so that it again could generate income. A taxpayer has no Constitutional right to force the government to negotiate terms.

3. The Service can attach *any* property owned by the taxpayer. If he owns insurance on his own life, the I.R.S. can attach the cash surrender value.

A taxpayer must know what to do promptly if the I.R.S. seizes assets. If the Service, accidentally or otherwise, takes over a taxpayer's property while it is in the hands of a third party (for example, goods shipped on consignment or machinery in the hands of the manufacturer for repair), the taxpayer must file suit to recover its property within nine months from the date of seizure.

If you owe money, there is no limit on how much of your property the I.R.S. can tie up. Liens and attachments properly can be applied to all of a taxpayer's assets and rights.

Where an I.R.S. lien is placed upon a person's property for nonpayment of taxes, a court will not interfere. The taxpayer is supposed to pay the tax and, if it had been incorrect, to sue for a refund. But that can take a considerable amount of time, and the taxpayer, without the use of its property, may be out of business by the time a court eventually decides that no tax really had been owed in the first place.

If the I.R.S. places a lien upon a taxpayer's property, very frequently he will not be able to sell this encumbered property, even though in fact no tax had been owed.

4. As mentioned earlier in this chapter, fines can be imposed for attempted interference with the administration of the tax laws.

5. The government can impose a lien upon a taxpayer's property. Any purchaser will acquire the property subject to this lien. This will

effectively prevent its sale or at least have a very depressing effect upon the price.

6.   A transfer of taxpayer's property to someone else, even in the case of a *bona fide* sale, can be set aside as an attempt to defraud creditors, namely, the Internal Revenue Service.

7.   A taxpayer can be sued for amounts of tax, interest, and penalty which he owes. Court costs may be added to what the taxpayer eventually pays.

8.   A jeopardy assessment, as described in Chapter 7, "The Tyranny of Time," may be issued against a taxpayer.

9.   Where the Service believes that a taxpayer intends to flee the country while his tax liability still is unsettled, a writ can be obtained to prevent his departure unless he shows proof that he owes no taxes to the government. The writ may be served at an airport, steamship terminal, or anywhere else.

10.   Information unearthed by Revenue Agents may find its way to other governmental agencies which are interested in prosecuting violators of non-tax laws. For example, incriminating information may be supplied to the Department of Justice, the Federal Trade Commission, the Securities and Exchange Commission, and the like. The Internal Revenue Service has "treaties" with the various state tax commissions for the exchange of information. If it is learned that a taxpayer has filed willfully erroneous state sales tax returns, he may be charged with fraudulent use of the United States Postal Service.

It is not double jeopardy when one governmental investigatory agency discovers a theft or embezzlement and this fact is brought to the attention of the Internal Revenue Service to check out whether the perpetrator had reported what he had taken as income on his tax return.

11.   A taxpayer may be convicted of a crime because of evidence that has been *stolen* by the I.R.S. from some other party. As long as the government's "dirty tricks" had not been performed on the taxpayer but on someone else, his rights had not been violated, held the U.S. Supreme Court in 1980.

12.   It is nothing to be ashamed about if the I.R.S. examines your income tax return. It could happen to anybody, for example, because of random selection by a computer. But your business can be hurt seriously, perhaps fatally, if the Service notifies your customers or clients that your tax returns are being investigated for possible criminal violations of the law. One accountant asked a court to stop this practice in his case on the ground that tax returns and the information appearing upon them are con-

fidential under the law. But the statute permits disclosures of tax return information where it is necessary to obtain information not otherwise available for the determination of tax. And those I.R.S. letters to his customers stating that he was under investigation may properly have been sent within the routine duties of Revenue Agents trying to collect additional information, declared a 1980 decision.

13.   Where a joint federal income tax return has been filed by husband and wife, one spouse's unpaid taxes can be collected from the other joint signer of the return, except where the latter can show that he or she met the requirements for innocent spouse status, a subject which has been discussed earlier in this book.

The Fair Debt Collection Practices Act has banned certain harassing tactics by collection agencies, such as dunning debtors in their homes at weird hours. The Appropriation Act of 1980 specifically applies this new rule to the nation's largest collection agency, the Internal Revenue Service.

The Penalty of Owning Property Jointly

Jointly owned property is subject to Internal Revenue Service action only to the extent of the delinquent co-owner's interest. But the other co-owner or co-owners can be hurt in the Service's enforcement activities. Father and son jointly owned a garage and service station. In an attempt to collect unpaid taxes owed by the son, I.R.S. agents seized the premises, padlocked the place, and posted a sign announcing that these proceedings had been brought on because of the son's unpaid taxes. The father brought suit against the Revenue Agents, claiming that they had wrongfully excluded him from his own property (including tools in which the son had no interest), deprived him of the right to conduct his business, and defamed him by posting the seizure notice for customers to see even though it had not even been charged that *he* owned back taxes. He was completely unsuccessful. Jointly owned property of a delinquent taxpayer can be seized when one co-owner owes taxes, and the fact that the father's personal property happened to be inside the building did not prevent its being padlocked to ensure that the son's interest in jointly owned property stayed firmly in governmental hands until Junior's taxes were paid. The father's name was not considered to have been defamed in the seizure notice, for customers and the public at large could have noted that only the son's name was mentioned—providing that anyone actually read the small print on the sign.

Cooperate with a Revenue Agent—But Not Too Much

It is advisable for a taxpayer to cooperate with a Revenue Agent. It has been mentioned earlier in this chapter that an uncooperative attitude may be equated with fraud or an attempt to interfere with the administration of the tax laws. Certainly it arouses the suspicions of a Revenue Agent, causing him to dig more deeply and perhaps to call in more aggressive members of his team.

But a taxpayer should not cooperate with a Revenue Agent to an unreasonable extent. Lavish entertaining, or even modest gifts, may be regarded as bribes. Even if no one else is present when a taxpayer or his representative gives something of value to a tax examiner, the latter is required to report the incident to his superiors, lest he in turn be accused of accepting a bribe or participating in a conspiracy to defraud the government.

Interest

Interest is charged on taxes not paid on or before their due date, even if an extension of time for filing had been granted. Penalty for failure to pay taxes may be waived upon a showing of reasonable cause, as discussed earlier in this chapter. But this waiver does not extend to interest on the unpaid amount.

The rate of interest on tax deficiencies is set once a year by the Internal Revenue Service. It is based upon banks' prime interest rates to their best clients at that time. The same rate is used if it is the government which must pay interest, such as when tax has been overpaid.

On February 1, 1980, the interest rate became 12%, to be effective through February 1, 1982.

Interest is allowed on refunds at the same rate, provided the payments were made in good faith and in fulfillment of a specific legal duty to pay what is owing. No interest is owed to a taxpayer on voluntary payments made where his tax liability had not been determined in accordance with what he believed to be the facts. For example, a person might deliberately overpay his taxes in order to have an assured interest payment at what he considers to be a good rate. Or a person might deliberately overpay his taxes so that he can show a federal tax return with substantial income to a creditor, with the intention of filling a refund claim for overpaid tax and interest as soon as the loan is granted on the basis of this overstated income.

If a person is entitled to a refund, no interest will be paid if the refund is made within forty-five days of the due date of the return, determined without reference to any extensions of filing time or, if a return is filed after the due date, within forty-five days of the date filed. If the refund is not made within this forty-five day period, interest will be paid from the due date of the return or from the date of filing, whichever is later.

A taxpayer may object to the amount of the interest which he is charged on a tax deficiency, claiming that if the return had been audited promptly, any interest charged would be small. There may indeed be a temptation to raise such a protest, where a Revenue Agent was called away from an audit for other investigatory chores or where the examiner went on the sick list for an extended period. Such protests are unavailing. Underpayment of income tax liability calls for interest from the taxpayer. Otherwise he would have had the use of money belonging to the government without charge. If tax has been underpaid, the interest is owed regardless of why the bill was so late in arriving.

As mentioned in another connection earlier in this chapter, a taxpayer may be paying what in other instances would be regarded as usurious interest. If property is seized and sold by the Internal Revenue Service for nonpayment of taxes, the delinquent taxpayer can get back his property from the purchaser by redeeming it within 120 days of the sale at the purchase price plus interest at the rate of 20% per year.

9.
Tax Traps—How Not to Let the Tax Cat Out of the Bag

Tax guides and instructions advise one about *what to do* in order to file federal income tax returns correctly and to avoid trouble with the Internal Revenue Service. Of equal importance is the generally ignored subject of *what not to do*. The tax law is strewn with traps and pitfalls which can make compliance with the requirements, or proof of what must be substantiated, unnecessarily difficult if not impossible. In addition, a taxpayer's own words or acts can contradict what he has stated in his tax return. This chapter will consider these problems. Evidence will be given in support of this essential advice: Never underestimate a Revenue Agent.

A Federal Agent's Opinion Is Only That

It was shown in Chapter 1 that the Internal Revenue Service is not bound by what its representatives say if the law is to the contrary or if the representative exceeds his authority. In addition, the Service may change its mind or revoke its own ruling at any time, even retroactively. In one decision, a judge announced that he was "perturbed when asked to subscribe to a thesis that the government's solemn word is as nothing." Unfortunately for taxpayers, that is what not infrequently happens. Only Congress can write a tax law, and only a court can say what the law means. A taxpayer is left in helpless perplexity when two courts of equal standing interpret a tax question in different ways. Even the United States Supreme Court has been known to reverse itself on a tax decision several years after it first interpreted a particular question.

An agreement made by a Revenue Agent with a taxpayer may be overturned by higher authority in the same office or in Washington.

The Internal Revenue Service is not bound by statements made by other government agencies. The Federal Farm Loan Board announced in its circulars that its bonds were exempt from federal income tax. An individual who purchased such bonds in reliance upon this statement (why should he have doubted it?) received a rude shock when the I.R.S. taxed him upon interest. But the Supreme Court held that the Farm Loan Board's opinion could not be relied upon in a federal income tax matter.

A person should read carefully anything which a person identifying himself as a Revenue Agent presents for signature. One individual posing as a Revenue Agent informed an elderly woman that he was investigating two local banks in which she had deposits and he wished permission to examine her accounts, which might have been subjected by bank personnel to unauthorized use. Her eyesight was poor and she did not understand until too late that actually she was empowering him to withdraw her funds. He did.

The Burden of Proof

Except in a fraud matter, a taxpayer has the burden of proof in virtually every type of tax situation in which he is likely to find himself. Being correct, such as in the right to take a deduction, is not enough. The taxpayer has to *prove* that he is correct, unlike the customary situation where a person is considered to be innocent until proven guilty.

Proving that one is correct in what he has stated on a tax return can be very difficult if not impossible, should the necessary records be destroyed by fire or flood, or if they are discarded prematurely, or if there has been some such event as vandalism or theft. Sometimes a person believes that something can be proven if necessary by the testimony of a highly credible party, who subsequently moves away or otherwise becomes unavailable, or who dies. Records in the possession of even the Internal Revenue Service may disappear or be destroyed by casualty, but the taxpayer is not relieved of his burden of proof.

One businessperson maintained a tax diary in which he made daily entries of travel, lodging, and entertainment expenses in connection with his work as a salesman. The diary admittedly met all substantiation requirements of the tax law. During an audit, the I.R.S. requested him to mail the diary to its nearest office, as the small size of the book made it difficult to copy. He did so, but it got lost somewhere along the line, either by the United States Postal Service or by the I.R.S. Without substantiation, it was held in the court's decision, his business expenses could be disallowed by the tax examiners. But the court permitted him to deduct any expenditures which he could credibly reconstruct. That, alas, did not cover everything shown in the diary, which, judging by the diaries that he had kept for other years, must have been maintained meticulously.

An exemption authorized by the law can be forfeited because of an uncooperative dependent. If you would claim an exemption for a dependent, frequently it is necessary to get some information from that party. Without some figures from the person, the exemption is apt to be lost. ("Now don't you be snooping into my affairs, Junior.") One individual contributed towards his mother's support. She had no income except Social Security benefits of an amount not known to her son. Without knowledge of what these amounts were, he could not prove that he had provided more than half of her support, as required by law. This often happens where parents are separated and relations between them could be characterized as unfriendly. The father contributes a substantial amount to the support of the child, but without knowing how much someone else may be contributing (perhaps petty cash), the father is not entitled to the dependency exemption which in fact he has earned.

An individual has the Constitutional right to remain silent. Should he avail himself of this time-honored privilege, however, he may not be able to meet this burden of proof in a tax matter.

A person may be hurt by presumption or coincidence if he cannot prove what *didn't* happen. Possession of cash, or a large bank account, or any form of unexplained wealth is accepted as proof of unreported taxable income where an individual has possible sources of income which could be taxed (for example, he runs a store) and he cannot prove that the money actually represented something of a nontaxable nature, such as the repayment of an old loan or the receipt of a gift or an inheritance.

Proof of Mailing

A taxpayer may be called upon to prove that he filed a tax return, refund claim, or other document on time. If the postmark is missing or illegible (which obviously is not his fault), he cannot prove the time of mailing, nor can he do so if the envelope cannot be found.

A person may fail to comply with the requirement of timely filing or protesting when he has not received a communication requiring prompt attention. In one case, a person received a communication from the Internal Revenue Service which had been almost completely destroyed by the malfunction of a Postal Service machine. Not knowing what the letter was about, he was unable to reply in time; but inasmuch as the communication had been addressed to his last known (and present) home by the I.R.S., he was deemed to have received it, and the failure to reply was his. If a person moves, he may be called upon to prove that he sent a change of address notice to the Internal Revenue Service or to the local post office. If he cannot do that, he will be held responsible for failure to comply with a letter which may never have reached him.

There have been instances of destruction of United States post offices, even in major cities. Under such circumstances communications could be prevented from being delivered on time, if at all, and postmarked dates would be unavailable.

Lack of Proper Tax Forms

If an individual is required to file a certain tax form or schedule on a particular date, he is not excused by reason of the fact that he never was provided with the proper form. Nor is he excused if the Internal Revenue Service is unable to supply its own forms when needed.

In one case, an individual asked an I.R.S. office for a certain form which had to be filed by a particular date. Through carelessness, a Service clerk gave him an incorrect form, which the taxpayer filed on time. Inasmuch as he had not submitted the *proper* form on time, he was treated as though he had failed to meet the requirement that the necessary document be filed by the date specified. That he had requested the proper form and the error actually was that of an I.R.S. clerk made no difference whatsoever.

Failure to Receive Information from Payor

A person may not rely upon his employer, a bank, the payor of interest or dividends, or some other source to advise him of what to report to the Internal Revenue Service as income. Failure to receive such information, or the correct information, is no excuse for failure to report it properly.

Payors of most forms of income are obliged to report amounts of fixed or determinable income to the Internal Revenue Service each year, with a copy to be sent to the payee for information in the preparation of his own federal income tax return. Amounts below specified figures, depending upon the nature of the payment, are not *required* to be reported to the Service by the payor. But a taxpayer is not justified in thinking that nothing was reported because the amount reported to him was less than this requirement. If one fails to report income because he did not receive a copy of the payor's report to the I.R.S., and he thereupon assumes that the payment was never reported because it did not have to be, he can find himself in the unenviable position of having failed to report income which the government knows about already. A taxpayer in the utmost good faith may fail to report income because he hasn't been reminded of it by the payor.

Don't Agree with the I.R.S. Too Quickly

A taxpayer may feel that it is useless to fight higher authority or that it is not worth the aggravation to protest or that he is a person who hates controversy and simply wants to get on to the other business of life. So when a Revenue Agent questions something on the income tax return, or a deficiency notice is received from the Internal Revenue Service, the taxpayer immediately agrees to the I.R.S. position.

But that spirit of quick cooperation may achieve an effect just the opposite of terminating matters quickly and amicably. According to *I.R.S. Audit Technique Handbook for Internal Revenue Agents*. "Hasty agreement to adjustments and undue concern about immediate closing of the case may indicate a more thorough examination is needed." Consequently, a taxpayer's spirit of cooperation and good fellowship may be an invitation to a Revenue Agent really to dig into a tax return and its documentary substantiation. "What doesn't he want me to find?"

In the case of a person whose income is large enough or complex enough to call for annual federal income tax audits, ready acceptance of any deficiency the Service chooses to impose predictably will create a situation where I.R.S. personnel come to believe that the person will pay *any* disallowed amount without appeal to the courts. It may be advisable for this person to litigate an assessment from time to time, perhaps only once, simply to avoid giving the impression that he, for his own reasons, wants to stay out of court at any price.

Retroactive Changes in the Law

There may be several ways in which you could structure a transaction, with different federal income tax treatment. But if the tax law is changed after your transaction takes place but in the same year, you can't argue that your transaction should not be taxed under a rule which did not even exist when the matter took place. That you would have cast the transaction in a different form had you known the law would be changed retroactively is irrelevant, held the U.S. Supreme Court in a 1981 decision.

Closing Agreement

Just because a Revenue Agent or other Internal Revenue Service employee tells you that your tax return has been accepted as filed or that some particular point he had questioned appears to have been handled correctly, do not throw away your records or otherwise consider the matter closed. Even if you sign an acceptance of a tax deficiency or overassessment, it can be reopened by the I.R.S. at any time until the statute of limitations runs out. This can lead to unfortunate results, such as it would if you had yielded on some point on which you believed you were absolutely correct in return for a particular Service concession which now is withdrawn. When a matter is reopened (actually, when the settlement is revoked), a person is in the awkward position of trying to justify a point on which he had already conceded.

Actually, any understanding with the Internal Revenue Service at any level is subject to repudiation by higher authority until the statute of limitations closes the taxable year involved. In only one instance is an understanding really the end of the matter: when a *closing agreement* is signed by both parties. But there is no substitute for the genuine product. After an examination, one taxpayer and the I.R.S. representative executed Form 4589, entitled "Income Tax Audit Changes," which has been discussed previously. But fifteen months later, the Commissioner of Internal Revenue replied that *he* had not agreed. A closing agreement, on Forms 906 or 866, must be signed both by the taxpayer and by the Commissioner or somebody else designated by him, such as a Regional Commissioner. Even if a closing agreement has been signed by both parties, it can become null and void if the I.R.S. can show that it was induced to sign by the taxpayer's fraud or substantial misstatement of a material fact.

Purchases for Cash

A person may make purchases of property or services for cash. This can save financing charges; it may be the means of paying a lower price. But when it comes to meeting the burden of proof required by the Internal Revenue Service in many situations, lack of a cancelled check can result in tax disadvantage. For example, if jewelry is lost by reason of fire or theft, deduction requires the establishment of *cost*. The Service has been held to be justified in taking the position that without proof of cost, the figure of zero must be used. If property is sold, recognition of taxable gain or loss depends upon computation of the difference between cost and realization, the taxpayer having the burden of proving the former. When a gift is made, the recipient's basis for determining gain or loss upon a subsequent sale is the donor's cost.

A credit card, despite claims in the advertisements of sponsors, may prove nothing for tax purposes. For example, in the case of business entertainment, the name of a restaurant, the date, and the amount spent does not meet the substantial requirements of contemporary recording of who was entertained and the business purpose for the expenditure.

Cash purchases may cause serious tax problems. If a person pays cash in a situation in which checks are customary, such as the purchase of inventory or the payment of a substantial medical bill, there can be implications of attempt to help the payee to evade the federal income tax law. There may even be involvement in a conspiracy action.

Transactions Entered into for Profit

In most instances, expenses are deductible only in the case of transactions entered into for profit. Losses similarly are deductible only in such a situation. An individual has the burden of proving that one of these indeed was the situation. This can be difficult in the case of an activity usually engaged in for pleasure, such as coin collecting.

Failure to list your trade or business correctly can forfeit a tax deduction. A person may deduct trade or business expenses. Or he may claim education expenses as related to his present trade or business. But such a deduction can be disallowed as personal if the space "Your occupation" on Page 1 of the federal income tax Form 1040 fails to show that same trade or business, according to a 1980 case.

If an activity, such as farming, is conducted in what one court referred to as "an unbusinesslike fashion," losses may be disallowed on the ground that if this really had been an activity entered into for profit, normal business practices would have been followed: the keeping of careful acquisition and expense records, consultation with parties knowledgeable in the field, subscriptions to professional magazines and services, efforts to eliminate unprofitable items or lines, regular review of how the enterprise is faring financially. A person has the burden of proving that he expected to make a profit, even if things didn't work out that way. In the language of one decision, "If a taxpayer sincerely and in good faith hopes and expects to make a profit, that is sufficient despite the fact that others may have testified that there is no reasonable expectation of making a profit.'' But he cannot demonstrate his sincerity without proof of credible nature.

Education expenses as such are not deductible. The expenses are deductible if they can be shown to be directly related to the maintenance of one's present job or the sharpening of his business skills. A retired accountant, apparently in an effort to keep his mind occupied with something stimulating, undertook a course of study in the field which most interested him: accounting. But he was not permitted to deduct his expenses, for they were not related to the business in which he then was engaged, which was nothing. He could not even argue that he intended to resume his former business of being an accountant, for there was no evidence that he expected to discontinue his retirement.

Sale of Stock Back to Employers

Under most circumstances, if a shareholder sells stock back to the corporation which issued it at a time when there are corporate earnings and profits, this income will be regarded as a fully taxable dividend to the seller and not capital gain. One of the few exceptions to this rule occurs when the shareholder sells *all* of his stock back to the corporation. But in order to avoid dividend treatment on this sale, no stock can be retained by his spouse, parents, children, or grandchildren.

Even if these relatives continue to hold stock, what the seller receives from the corporation will not be taxed as a dividend if he ceases to have any interest in the corporation as officer, employee, or director. A frequent trap here is that after a person retires and sells his stock back to the company, he may be persuaded to make his experience available to the business by staying on as a part-time employee or director. Then the income from the sale will be taxable as a dividend.

In the case of a closely-held corporation, frequently there is a requirement that if any shareholder retires or otherwise leaves the company, he must sell his stock back to the corporation. But if he accepts designation as a director, which generally is regarded as a compliment and an honor, the income from his sale of stock will be treated as a dividend.

Economic Benefits as Dividends

If a person owns stock in a corporation, any economic benefit which he receives from the company can be treated as a taxable dividend if there are earnings and profits large enough to pay a dividend. So if a share-holder makes use of corporate assets, such as a company car or recreation facilities, he has taxable income based upon the value of what he receives or uses. Should an executive who happens to own stock in the company have the use of a company car, he must be able to prove what percentage of the car was for business purposes. If he is unable to make an acceptable allocation, the Internal Revenue Service may tax the full, or a major portion of, the value of the car's use to him as a dividend, as the right to use corporate assets for personal purposes.

If a stockholder's son makes use of a company vehicle, this can be taxed to the shareholder as a dividend, for Junior was allowed to use corporate assets only because of his father's ownership of stock. To avoid dividend treatment, the father should advise the employees not to let his son use company property.

To be taxed as a dividend, the economic advantage or payment need not be called a dividend or formally "declared," despite what the laws of the state of incorporation say on the subject. To be taxed as a dividend, the payment or benefit need not be made on a proportionate basis. Thus if one shareholder is permitted to buy company property at a bargain price, he has a taxable dividend, although the other shareholders received nothing.

Economic Benefits as Compensation

When a person is an executive or other employee of a business enter-prise, anything of economic benefit he receives from the company, any payment the company makes for his benefit, is regarded as taxable com-pensation unless the tax law specifically makes an exception. One of the few exceptions is a corporation's payment of premiums on group term life insurance to provide an employee with not more than $50,000 of coverage. So if an executive is permitted to buy the company's product at a discount, or to purchase last year's executive car at a price substan-tially less than market value, he has received taxable income to the extent of the bargain.

If an executive's entertainment expenses are paid by his employer, but it cannot be proven that the expenditures were for business rather than personal purposes, the executive can be taxed upon the amount of these expenses as additional compensation. So it is up to him to keep careful records to show that the business rather than he profited from the enter-tainment, or he will be taxed.

Nothing Is Too Small

A taxpayer may realize the need for proper records and other forms of proof. But he may believe that in the case of small items, there is no practical reason to be so particular. If an expenditure for medical costs, contributions, interest, business entertainment, or anything else is worth deducting, it is worth the trouble of substantiating. As one court stated in an opinion, "For tax purposes, there is no rule excusing a taxpayer from paying deficiencies which are relatively immaterial." This means that anything on the tax return which may be questioned should be documented.

In the words of one decision, "Contrary to [the taxpayer's] argument, the regulations do not dispense with the recordkeeping requirements for [entertainment] expenditures of less than $25 except for the need of keeping receipts."

It has been mentioned in another connection that if the Internal Revenue Service imposes additional tax because income had been understated, should *any* part of the deficiency have been the result of fraud, the entire deficiency is subject to the fraud penalty. The same treatment may be applied in the case of negligence. So if a person takes a chance on a small item which seems to be too insignificant to be zeroed in on by the tax examiners, he is risking a penalty on a deficiency which may be primarily the result of good faith or arithmetical errors.

The Danger of Taking Risks on an Income Tax Return

A businessperson has to be prepared to take risks. But taking chances on your income tax return is a gamble that involves more than disallowances of improperly handled items. If reported taxable income is too small, here is what can happen: (1) The unreported taxable income must be paid with interest (deductible). (2) There is a penalty (non-deductible) of ½ of 1% for each month of the nonpayment, up to 25% of the unpaid tax. (3) If any part of the underpayment is attributable to negligence, there can be a 5% penalty on the *entire amount* of any resultant tax deficiency. (4) There is a 50% penalty on the entire amount of any tax deficiency if any part of it is the result of fraud. (5) Mishandling of an item in one year can lead the I.R.S. to examine the returns of all prior years not yet closed by the statute of limitations to see whether there can be similar disallowances, in the domino manner, for those years. (6) If any part of a tax deficiency involves an item on which there was fraud, there is no statute of limitations, and the I.R.S. can examine critically whatever appears there at any future time. (7) Improper handling of an item can poison the entire climate of what had been a routine and amicable examination. From now on, nothing may be taken for granted. The Revenue Agent may conclude, perhaps wrongfully, that here is a return on which a line-by-line audit would be productive. He may have assigned to work with him an especially tough examiner to help him put the suspected taxpayer through the wringer.

Signing an Incompleted Tax Return

Sometimes a person who expects to be away on business or vacation, or in a hospital, at the time when his federal income tax return is to be filed, signs a tax form presented to him by his accountant or a trusted employee before any figures have been inserted. This can result in a fraud penalty, because the return is characterized as one signed with willful disregard of the accuracy of the figures (non-existent in this situation) contained therein. Certainly the person knew the return was incorrect when he signed it if there were no numbers inserted.

A similar fraud situation arises if an individual is an officer of a corporation, the tax return of which he signs "in blank" because he will not be in town by the time the return is ready for his signature.

Don't Volunteer

When a Revenue Agent questions the tax treatment of some item on a tax return, a person may be tempted to justify his handling of the matter by declaring, "Why, that's the way I've always handled it." The predictable result will be attempted disallowance of the item for all years not yet closed by the statute of limitations, customarily three. If there is a question as to whether tax treatment is proper for this year, the worst thing you can do is to refer to other years. As a rule, a Revenue Agent will not look at tax returns except for the year or years specifically assigned to him. But if you bring to his specific attention improperly handled treatment in other years, he can scarcely shut his eyes to this.

Refund Claims

No one is required to pay more federal income taxes than he owes, obviously, and if taxes have been overpaid, he is entitled to a refund if demand is made in proper form within the permissible time. But frequently a refund claim is a trap, so a taxpayer is in a quandary if he later discovers that a proper deduction was not taken or that income was not actually reportable for a certain year.

Here is the first risk. Filing a claim is apt to be like opening Pandora's box. You never know what is going to be found. In one case, a taxpayer believed that his tax had been overpaid by $972.48. But by the time the Internal Revenue Service had reexamined the return and found other items to disallow, and the court had reviewed the matter with the result that some other taxpayer shortcomings had been unearthed, the bill amounted to $27,569.15. A court may be much tougher than the I.R.S. was. And when a tax return is opened for one purpose, all sorts of other things can pop up.

If a second refund claim for the same taxable year is filed before the first one is acted upon, be sure to repeat all of the facts which appeared in the first claim. Otherwise it may be considered that the second claim, which actually covers an additional item, is superseding the first one, and what had been claimed there no longer is being sought.

A successful refund claim can result in a net additional tax assessment. A refund claim could lead the I.R.S. to scrutinize that year's return carefully. Even though this claim proves to be justified, other previously unsuspected items now may prove to have been handled incorrectly. Result: the Service increases tax liability for more than the amount of the proper refund claim.

Don't let high interest rates tempt you to wait to the last moment to claim a refund. One day's tardiness, to get that high interest for as long as possible, can forfeit the entire refund if the claim is late. It was stated in a 1980 decision: "While the Court is not in the business of giving tax advice, it does seem appropriate under the circumstances to comment that [taxpayers] assume a considerable risk in utilizing this sort of savings program. If such a plan is utilized, the taxpayer should make sure that his/her return/claim for refund is mailed to *and* received by the I.R.S. before the . . . claim period expires."

When your tax return is being audited, an indicated error in your favor may be disclosed. Sometimes a Revenue Agent will say that this adjustment will be taken care of by his office and that you do not have to file a claim. Do it anyway. The matter could be overlooked by the I.R.S.

A Court May Be Stricter Than the I.R.S.

If the Internal Revenue Service disagrees with a taxpayer's treatment of some item on the return, the latter may feel that he should let a court decide the proper liability. After all, it may be thought, the worst that can happen is that the court will agree with what the Service has proposed to do.

But the court does not have to agree with either party. It is a body without obligation to accept either of the points of view presented. In one case, the question was valuation of stock for tax purposes. The taxpayer had used a figure of $10 a share for the valuation which was to be taxed. When the I.R.S. increased this to $25, the taxpayer sought relief in court. Frequently a judge will come up with a compromise figure, but here the court decided that the valuation properly was $37 a share.

Handling Your Own Case

A taxpayer is entitled to represent himself in any tax litigation. Some persons do this, especially in the small claims division of the United States Tax Court, where the rules are not so technical as they are in other courts. Even here, however, a taxpayer who is not thoroughly familiar with requirements as to evidence and procedure is apt to be at a great disadvantage when confronted by an experienced government attorney. As the court declared in one case, "With a strong regard for the right of any taxpayer to represent himself in an action before this Court, it is nevertheless our observation that [the taxpayer], in a case such as this where a reasonably large deficiency is in dispute, would have been well advised to place the presentation of his case in the hands of an experienced and well trained practitioner."

But a lawyer, however fine his qualifications in his own area of specialization, may have little knowledge of tax matters, having devoted his practice for many years to patents and trademarks, or some other particularized area. A taxpayer can be hurt by his attorney's unfamiliarity with taxes. In one case, a taxpayer turned over a deficiency notice from the Internal Revenue Service to a lawyer, with a request to arrange to have the Tax Court review the matter before any tax had to be paid. Instead of addressing the communication to the United States Tax Court in Washington, as should have been done, the lawyer sent it to "IRS District Court, San Francisco," the city where the taxpayer was located and sent his tax returns. Ultimately this request for a hearing reached the Tax Court in Washington, but well after the time limit permitted for an appeal which would have suspended the payment of taxes. That court declared it was powerless to hear a belated appeal, "regardless of the cause for its not being filed within the required period."

In another situation of the same type, the taxpayer was represented by a lawyer who had had considerable experience in federal income tax matters. That, however, had been many years ago, and meanwhile he had specialized in other areas of the law. The attorney sent the request for a hearing on the tax deficiency to the Board of Tax Appeals in Washington, the name used by the court during the attorney's contacts with it. But the name had been changed to the United States Tax Court in 1944, some twenty-three years earlier, and the post office returned the envelope as undeliverable because the postal personnel no longer were familiar with the long-abandoned name. Re-mailing to the renamed court was too late to permit an appeal in this manner. Had the taxpayer handled his own appeal, he, being totally unfamiliar with the procedure, doubtless would have checked the name and address where the petition was to be sent, instead of relying upon memory of the way it used to be.

Contributions

Contributions within the permissible limits are deductible only when made to donees included on the Treasury Department's list of organizations, contributions to which are deductible for tax purposes. The organization's name, however respectable, is no assurance that approval had been granted. In addition, the list is being revised constantly, and the mere fact that an organization *was* listed at one time does not imply that it was on the approval list at the time of the contribution.

Contributions to approved charitable, religious, and educational organizations are deductible up to certain stipulated ceilings. But an organization can lose this preferential status, most commonly because discrimination is practiced. A private school seeking to obtain or to retain tax-exempt status must publicize its racially nondiscriminatory admissions policy. It isn't enough for a school to state publicly that it has never denied admission to a black person, for perhaps none had ever applied.

Frequently persons receive solicitations of funds from organizations, which state in their letters or literature that "Contributions are deductible for tax purposes." Obviously such a statment is not binding on the Internal Revenue Service, which has its own ideas on the subject. In addition, contributions are deductible only to the extent that in aggregate they do not exceed a stipulated percentage of the donor's adjusted gross income for that year, the percentage depending upon the nature of the contribution. Clearly the organizations which say that "Contributions are deductible for tax purposes" have no way of knowing what a donor's adjusted gross income or other contributions amount to in a particular year, If, because of abnormally low income in the taxable year, a donor's contributions exceed the permissible percentage of his adjusted gross, the excess is not deductible. There can be a carryover of unused contributions to later years, but of course there is no certainty that the carryover can ever be used up, this depending upon circumstances in subsequent years.

If a donor receives anything in return for his contribution, it is not regarded as a contribution for tax purposes. For example, an individual may give a sum of money to a tax-exempt museum with no thought of receiving anything in return. But he is sent copies of magazines and books which are sold to outsiders by the museum, he is given a membership card which other persons pay for, he is given tickets to special events not open to the general public. What he has *contributed* to the tax-exempt organization may be whittled down to nothing. Actually what he was given gratuitously may have been of no interest or value to him. Even if a benefit is extremely small and is not in cash, the organization forfeits its exempt status and the contributor his tax deduction.

One form of contribution is not deductible for tax purposes, even when made to an unquestionably *bona fide* organization which is on the officially approved list. A contribution of one's own blood to a hospital, says the Internal Revenue Service, is not a deductible contribution because it does not represent *property*. It is regarded as a service. Such a ruling only fortifies the conclusion of many cynics that the I.R.S. does not place a very high value upon a taxpayer's life-blood.

Casualties

Casualty losses are deductible for federal income tax purposes, except for the first $100 of personal, nonbusiness property, but this refers only to losses which are not reimbursable by insurance or otherwise. If a person fails to seek reimbursement to which he is entitled, for whatever reason, he has no deductible casualty loss.

A trap is that a taxpayer may believe that he has compelling reasons for not seeking reimbursement. For example, after a theft loss has been sustained, it may be learned that the perpetrator was an employee or acquaintance who, for reasons beyond his own control, was in a very serious financial crisis and simply had to have money for an operation. But in such a situation, the Internal Revenue Service predictably will claim that the taxpayer made a gift out of sympathy. Perhaps the taker of property is not in position to make reimbursement, but the tax law means reimbursement *from any source*. It may be that his family would be willing to make good the loss so as to avoid disgrace to a relative. Be sure you have really tried all possible ways of getting reimbursement before claiming a casualty loss deduction. The I.R.S. will require proof of this.

A taxpayer may fail to report a theft or comparable loss to the police because of a sense of futility. There were no known witnesses, so how could money or other property be recovered even if a prompt recital of facts to the local constabulary had taken place? Don't fall into this trap. If you did not regard what happened as a casualty, the I.R.S. will say, you didn't establish that a theft really had taken place. Conceivably, the alleged theft loss was merely the idea of somebody else at a much later date, suggested as a way of gaining you a tax deduction. Documentation of a deduction should be *contemporary*.

Dealing with the Internal Revenue Service

An individual should avoid any mention of how experienced he is in tax matters or what taxation courses he has mastered during his discussions with the Revenue Agent who is examining his return. This would suggest that, because of the taxpayer's admitted great familiarity with the subject, any understatement of taxable income on the return must have been the result of a deliberate attempt to evade taxes known to be due rather than simple unawareness or careless error. Such a person as he has painted himself to be would not have under-reported income or added expenses in that manner, except in an effort to commit fraud.

After completion of a tax examination, a person should avoid praising the Revenue Agent's abilities to his superior, the group supervisor. Such praise can suggest to higher authority that the agent was too lenient or, for one reason or another, that he permitted improper tax treatment to pass without challenge. A predictable response of the agent's superior would be to send around a much more suspicious, tougher type to review the work which had been done.

It's Risky to Keep Computations of What the I.R.S. May Disallow on Audit

A taxpayer may wish to avoid unpleasant surprises that could result from any increases in taxable income as the result of an examination of the return. If the Service, in going through a taxpayer's records and work-papers, finds computations that show the additional tax that would result from "correction" of any items, predictably the Service will make these changes, as even management had its doubts as to the correctness of its position. This could even result in the imposition of a fraud penalty if there was evidence that management *knew* that tax should have been paid on a certain transaction but it wasn't.

The "No Change" Letter

After a tax examination, the I.R.S. may send you a "no change" let-ter, such as this actual one: "Dear Taxpayer: You will be pleased to know that our examination of your tax return for the above periods shows no change is required in the tax reported. Your returns are accepted as filed." On your next audit, something is disallowed although it has been handled in precisely the same manner as in the "no change" year(s). That "no change" letter for one or more years doesn't assure you of the same treatment next year. So reliance on such a letter can cause you to proceed blissfully to make an error without bothering to check out the situation with a competent advisor.

The Biggest Trap of All

The most serious of all possible tax traps is *complacency*. Don't as-sume that your intuitive response to any problem or question is the correct one. Don't assume that unsubstantiated or dubious items will be accepted at face value. And *do not underestimate the Revenue Agent*. He or she probably is much better trained than you imagine. Even if he is not highly experienced, he has a back-up team of thoroughly experienced, knowl-edgeable, and persistent investigators. Some are specialists.

Here are some actual examples of Revenue Agent ingenuity which cost complacent taxpayers dearly:

• Unexplained wealth was identified by one taxpayer as a gift from his mother. But it was discovered by a resourceful Revenue Agent that he had claimed her as a dependent for the same year on an application to the Selective Service Board in an effort to be classified as a hardship case.

• If the I.R.S. is not satisfied with the accuracy of a taxpayer's records, the Service can reconstruct taxable income in other ways, such as the net worth method. Here the Service must establish a taxpayer's opening and closing net worths with reasonable accuracy, and any unexplained increase at the end of the period, taking living expenses into account, is deemed to be taxable income. The problem for the I.R.S. is to establish opening net worth where the taxpayer's records are untrustworthy. In one case, the taxpayer did that chore for the Service himself without knowing it. At about the time when net worth was to be established by the government, he filed an application for a bank loan, to which he attached a net worth statement he'd prepared. A Revenue Agent found this at the bank.

• Periodic alimony payments set or approved by a divorce court are deductible, within a specified framework. But one Revenue Agent discovered that a kindly ex-husband voluntarily had increased these payments so that his former wife could keep up with higher living costs. The increased amounts were not deductible, not having been court-approved.

• An individual's claim for dependency exemptions for his three children depended on whether he had provided more than half of their support in that taxable year. The Internal Revenue Service ascertained, in a 1978 case, that the Massachusetts Department of Public Welfare had provided more of their support funds than he did.

• A taxpayer listed three children on his income tax return as dependents. A tax investigation revealed no record of "the twins." They were not recognized, but fraud was.

• A businessperson can deduct unreimbursable travel and entertainment expenses only when they are recorded in a prescribed manner contemporaneously. One salesman dutifully itemized his expenses for a year, about a dozen pens having been used for the purpose. But microscopic examination showed that the same ink had been used at the same time for all of the entries.

• A commercial traveler claimed a mileage deduction for the business use of his car, based upon monthly mileage travel books which he kept. A Revenue Agent was permitted to slash the figures by about 40% because the mileage claimed far exceeded the numbers shown on the odometer.

• A businessperson had a credit card issued in his name as a company executive, charges being borne by the business. An alert Revenue Agent discovered that the card was being used to make purchases by the executive's wife, who performed no business services. The amounts were taxed to him personally as a form of additional compensation.

• In checking an executive's business entertainment deductions, one Revenue Agent went to see some of the largest customers who had been "entertained." That was the first time any of them knew that they had been dined and wined handsomely. Result: disallowance of the entertainment expenses.

• A businessperson's deduction of expenses for entertaining customers was slashed by the Internal Revenue Service when a tax examiner visited several of the people whose entertainment had involved the most money. In response to the Revenue Agent's questions, the customers stated that they would have placed the same orders even if they had not been entertained. Those expenditures were regarded by the Service as not having been for the purpose of obtaining business, and a court agreed.

• An individual who had had a heart attack claimed that the cost of installing a mobile telephone in his car was solely to get medical assistance quickly if he was stricken while on the road. But a careful Revenue Agent found that the telephone number of this mobile unit was listed in the directory, and no reason could be given why a doctor would need to look up his number to call *him* for a checkup.

• A prominent musician claimed a contributions deduction of $350,000 for a gift of his manuscripts to a university library. But it was found that up to the time of the gift, he had had this collection insured for $1,500.

• A business deducted a $46,000 annual salary which was paid to the individual who kept the books. A considerable portion of this was disallowed as unreasonable compensation when a Revenue Agent questioned the individual and learned that he did not know the difference between the cash and the accrual methods, or between single and double entry accounting.

• A businessman claimed that his wife was his partner. But when a Revenue Agent came to the office by appointment to check the tax returns, the wife, who made a point of being present on this occasion, did not know the location of the ladies' room.

• A bus driver deducted the cost of his "uniform," which he had to wear while on duty. But when asked to display this clothing, it proved to be an ordinary conservative gray business suit, completely without insignia of any kind. Thus it did not meet the requirements of deductible uniform or special clothing: something which cannot be worn for ordinary social or street apparel.

• Commuting expenses are not deductible. But if a person incurs *additional* expenses in travelling between his home and his place of employment because of the necessity of carrying the tools of his trade to work, he may deduct this additional expense. One individual sought to deduct the costs of driving his car to work on the ground that the equipment he had to take along with him was too heavy to tote if he took the bus, as allegedly he would have done had it not been for this weighty encumbrance. Unfortunately for his story and the tax deduction, a suspicious Revenue Agent checked the bus schedules. He found that even if the taxpayer had not been burdened with tools, he would not have taken the bus, for there was nothing scheduled which could have gotten him to work at the required time.

• If a federal tax examiner seems to have a shifty look, that doesn't necessarily mean that he's an untrustworthy knave who can't look an honest taxpayer in the face. It's just that he has been programmed to look at other things. One Revenue Agent admired a photograph of a decedent during a visit to the executor, her husband. Where does that handsome necklace appear on the estate tax return's "Other Miscellaneous Property" schedule, wondered the examiner aloud. The embarrassed executor added in the value. That wasn't all that was added to the estate tax payable.

How Not to Let the Tax Cat Out of the Bag

At times, an individual contradicts by his own statements a statement or figures which he showed on his federal income tax return. Here are some actual examples:

• An individual may deduct expenses and losses in connection with an activity entered into for profit. One person was not permitted to deduct the costs he had incurred in the writing of books and pamphlets. When asked by a Revenue Agent why he had written these works, he replied, "The desire to be of use beyond gaining one's own needs is strong in everyone and I think it becomes stronger as the responsibility of self-support becomes lightened. This usefulness is the whole motive that I have in the . . . work." Thus, his assertion of a benevolent rather than a selfish motive cost him a tax deduction. In analyzing cases of this kind, one court said that judges are quick to find "the requisite greed." But here the taxpayer denied the requisite greed in writing, and his tax return suffered because his motive had not been to make money.

- A contractor attempted to deduct expenses of a chicken farm which he operated during his spare time. But his own books of account showed that it cost him an average of $65 per chicken to operate the farm. Deduction was denied, for his own records established that there was no reasonable expectation of carrying on this activity for profit.

- One person argued that omissions of income from his tax return were the result of ignorance, which should not result in penalty because he was not familiar with the requirements of the tax law. But this argument was destroyed because of a book he had written, entitled *Mind Your Business*. In a section entitled "Income Tax, Keeping Records," his readers were cautioned to "Be sure to keep all dates, amounts, and items with some degree of accuracy." The book suggested a simple and practical method of keeping records to avoid substantiation difficulties in tax matters. The author pointed out the very pitfalls which he later tried to say were unfamiliar matters to him.

- A bad debt is fully deductible only when it arose from a business transaction entered into with expectation of payment. One taxpayer was denied a deduction for unrepaid loans after he testified that "I really don't know why I made them."

- A taxpayer's returns could not be reconciled with his own records, so the Internal Revenue Service sought to tax him upon unexplained increases in his net worth. He claimed that the Service's computation of his net worth was improper and showed too high a figure at the year's end. But the Service produced a rather similar computation of his net worth which the taxpayer had prepared for his own purposes, which even bore his signature.

- A physician endeavored to support his federal income tax return by showing his cash receipts book. But many of the entries in this book contained apparently meaningless letters next to the figures. These actually were coded notations of what the figures really should have been. A Revenue Agent broke the code, and the physician was taxed upon what was revealed by his "secret" notations.

- One taxpayer sought to deduct law school tuition as a business expense, claiming that he had no intention of practicing law but merely wanted to have legal training to help him in his business. But on his application for admission to law school, in response to a question of why he was seeking to take up the study of law, he had replied that his sole purpose was to engage in full-time practice as an attorney. So the expenditures were disallowed, not being related to the maintenance of his existing job or business.

- A prominent industrialist argued that her failure to deduct withholding and Social Security taxes from employees' wages had not been a deliberate attempt to interfere with the administration of the tax laws, for she was not familiar with the withholding requirements. But it was brought out that she had published many articles denouncing the requirement that employers undergo the expense of being a collection agency for the government, and here she had stated emphatically that she never would comply with such a law.

An individual also may be convicted by his own actions if they are contrary to what he is arguing for tax purposes:

- One person claimed that he should not be penalized for failure to file federal income tax returns for several years. He showed that during this period he had been badly injured in an accident, he had been seriously ill, he had undergone surgery in three of the four years for which tax returns had not been filed. But the record showed that throughout this period, despite ill health and the knife, he had been going to his place of business regularly and consistently.

- A casualty loss is deductible only when the occurrence is sudden and unexpected. After his home had collapsed because of termite infestation of the underpinning, the owner claimed that this was a casualty which could not have been prevented because of its unexpectedness. But a Revenue Agent found a letter in the files in which an exterminator had warned that termites were at work and would have to be dealt with immediately or the building would collapse. The letter and its warning had not been acted upon by the taxpayer, so what happened could not be regarded as sudden and unexpected.

- One taxpayer argued that he should not be penalized for understatement of taxable income on his return because he did not know that an apparently simple transaction had complex tax involvements which he had interpreted incorrectly. But his accountant had written a letter warning him of the existence of this problem and suggesting that he write to the Internal Revenue Service for an opinion. The accountant's letter, which had been ignored, showed that the taxpayer was not unaware of the fact that a tax problem had to be considered.

10.
How to Be a Good Taxpayer

It is not only a matter of pride, but of common sense, to decide that if you are going to do something, you should do it well. It also is a matter of economics. Certainly this simple principle applies to being a taxpayer. Not only are you required to be one if the arithmetic so indicates. It is expensive in many ways not to be as good a taxpayer as possible.

What to Do

Here are twelve essential rules for being a good taxpayer:

1. *Know what is expected of you.* Although Congress and the Internal Revenue Service have poured forth oceans of words as to what a taxpayer must do, he really is on his own in applying this flood of printed material, as interpreted by thousands of court decisions, to his own particular situation each year. I.R.S. instruction sheets and pamphlets describe who must file an income tax return, when, where, and how. Beyond that, each taxpayer has to determine what he must do. He may ask the assistance of the Internal Revenue Service, lawyers and accountants, professional tax preparers, friends. But their aid is limited by being based on only the information he supplies or the questions he asks. It is up to the taxpayer to find out what this means himself or to ask a great many questions of his own. He must realize that in almost every type of situation, he has the burden of proof. All inflow is taxable unless he can establish that it is not. No deductions are permitted unless he can demonstrate his entitlement to them. Not only does he have to prove that what he has done is correct. Often he has the problem of negative proof, that is, showing that something did not happen or could not have taken place. For example, in claiming a casualty loss deduction, he must not only show that he did not receive reimbursement from an insurance company or other party, but also that he could not have obtained any offset to his loss even if he had tried in every possible way.

Reliance upon an expert does not relieve you of your obligations, for it is your signature at the bottom of the tax return and the expert is only helping (or harming) you. So you must be satisfied that the party upon whom you rely really is expert. And you must make a full disclosure to him of all of the facts and circumstances necessary to provide a proper response. The taxpayer has to know enough of the requirements to understand what "full disclosure" really includes. It may mean *everything*.

2. *Always behave as though your income tax return is going to be examined by the Internal Revenue Service.* A thoughtful taxpayer is scarcely likely to omit an income item or to claim an improper deduction if he believes that a Revenue Agent will review the return microscopically. He is unlikely to resolve doubts as to the tax treatment of items in his own favor if he believes this matter will be given The Eye, unless he first checks out the situation with someone who is knowledgeable in this area. *Assume that your return will be scrutinized minutely.* Then you are not likely to take unjustifiable risks on the gamble that your figures will go unquestioned. This means being in a position to prove everything that goes on the tax return, or would go on it except for some special reason or circumstances that you can show are permitted by the tax law.

Figures shown by you are not self-proving, and the necessary substantiation is a taxpayer's primary obligation. What you cannot prove is subject to the mercy of the Internal Revenue Service, which is not a charitable organization. The fact that your records were destroyed in a fire, or that the person who can testify as to what happened now is dead, will not be accepted as an excuse for lack of proof. In the words of one court decision, "difficulty or even impossibility of proof does not relieve [a taxpayer] of the burden." This means accumulation of back-up material when you prepare the tax return, for such data probably are available at that time. And it means keeping this material in a safe place, where you or your heirs can find it if it is needed. You may be able to justify what you say on your tax return, but can your heirs if you fail to leave the necessary records and papers where they can be found?

3. *Remember that Tax Day is not only April 15.* Because of the need to meet obligations of proof, April 15 can no longer be regarded as "Tax Day." Even where a person believes that he will use the zero bracket amount for deductions instead of itemizing, he may not know until his tax return is prepared which method will be more advantageous. This means accumulation of bills, receipts, cancelled checks, and all other forms of substantiation on a continuing basis. Typically, it may not be known until after the year's end whether you can claim a certain person as a dependent. Unless you keep current records of your payments to-

wards the support of the alleged dependent, you will not be able to determine whether you paid more than half of the support as required in order to qualify for this treatment. If you have a fire loss or other casualty, the necessary proof of the value of your house or car immediately after that event may be provided by a photograph, provided you remember to take it at once. When you sell securities or other property, it will be necessary to have proof not only of what you received, but also of what the property cost. It may take a considerable amount of time to gather reliable information about costs, particularly where you acquired property many years ago or obtained it by gift or inheritance. You can't wait until April 15 to do this.

4. *Answer all questions on the income tax form.* There are a number of questions on the federal income tax return requiring answers. For example, "Did you, at any time during the taxable year, have any interest in or signature or other authority over a bank, securities, or other financial account in a foreign country . . . ?" "Did you deduct expenses for an office in your home?" If any question goes unanswered, predictably the Internal Revenue Service computers which scan your return will flag it for attention, the very least of which is a request for a response. It is not a good idea to give the I.R.S. the invitation to ask a question. If the Service is obliged to ask you to answer one question, the revenue people will think of other questions to ask as well. These may not be so simple to answer, or so free of possible trouble. Courts have held that if any printed question on the tax return form is unanswered, the entire form is characterized as "No return." This means there will be triggered the various unpleasant consequences which accompany the non-filing of an income tax return that is required.

Businesspersons are asked if deduction was claimed for entertainment facilities, employees' families at conventions or meetings, employee or family vacations not reported on Form W-2. Similarly, in a number of instances, lines on the tax return call for more than the insertion of numbers. For example, the lines calling for "Credit for the elderly," "Credit for child care expenses," "Investment credit," and various others specify "attach Form . . ." In the case of cash contributions, donees and amounts must be listed. Statements are required for noncash contributions. Interest and dividend income amounting to more than $400 in each category must be itemized. If you are called upon to complete schedules which you saw fit to ignore on the tax return, Internal Revenue Service personnel will wonder why you preferred not to supply the information. One request or question will lead to another, with greater insistence by the questioner. Remember that your signature on the tax return form states that you declare, under penalties of perjury, that all schedules and statements are, to the best of your knowledge and belief, "complete." Missing answers or schedules belie this.

Having one's income tax return tabbed by a computer for further investigation is to be avoided. Nor is it a satisfactory experience to have to correspond with a computer, which does not understand replies that it has not been programmed to comprehend.

5. *Anticipate what a Revenue Agent will want to examine.* When you have that confrontation session with an I.R.S. examiner, you will want to get it over with as rapidly as possible. The Service has explained how you can speed up the process by having readily available certain pieces of paper.

"To help us complete the examination of your return, please include the following with your records:

"For real and personal property taxes:

1. Canceled checks or receipts for taxes paid.

2. If you sold or purchased real property, a copy of the settlement statement.

3. Identification of any special assessments deducted as taxes, and an explanation of their purpose.

"For sales tax:

1. Receipts for sales taxes paid on a car, motorcycle, motor home, truck, boat, airplane, mobile or prefabricated home, or building materials you bought to build a new home.

2. If you paid more sales tax on items listed above than the amount shown for your income in the Optional State Sales Tax Tables (See Form 1040 instructions), verification of purchases on which sales tax was paid."

6. *Keep updated inventories of your possessions, including original costs.* If any appraisals of your property have been made, keep them. Take frequent photographs of your home, inside and outside. Take pictures also of your car, valuable trees and shrubs, collectibles such as medals, works of art, furniture, musical instruments.

A listing of what you have invested in your property is of great importance in the case of fire or theft losses. Unfortunately, people who carefully compile such lists often place them in a desk drawer in the house, so that the listing will be destroyed in the same fire that makes the price inventory necessary to establish the amount of deductible casualty loss. Don't let the casualty loss include a tax deduction.

Securities transactions records are available at most stationery stores. These records provide space for entry of original cost, later assessments on stock or contributions to capital, stock dividends, partial liquidiations, spin-offs, exchanges, and the like. Columns are provided for the listing of serial numbers, which are of prime necessity in case securities are lost, stolen, or destroyed. These should be kept in one's safe-deposit box.

If a person has acquired shares in a particular corporation at different times and at different prices, gain or loss on a sale of some of the stock depends for tax purposes upon proper identification of shares. For example, if market prices have gone up, sale of shares having the highest cost will produce the lowest capital gain. But if the person can't prove precisely *which* purchases he is selling, the I.R.S. can compute gain as of the first shares to have been purchased were the first to be sold. A seller should identify which shares he is selling by the use of certificate numbers. This presents no particular problem if all of the shares had been purchased. The practical problem is greater if some of the shares had been acquired through stock dividends, stock splits, mergers, recapitalizations, and the like. But such record keeping is possible and constantly is being done. Because of failure to keep records by serial numbers, one taxpayer in a 1980 case was not permitted to compute tax liability on a sale as if the shares with the highest cost had been sold at that time.

7. *Make certain that your records are safe.* As mentioned throughout this book, the taxpayer in almost all situations has the burden of proving whatever is stated on his tax return. This he can't do if the substantiating documents and workpapers are not available when he needs them. One safeguard is never to let original papers get out of your possession. Insist that back-up material be examined in your presence, or provide photocopies instead. In 1980, taxpayers were placed in impossible substantiation positions in these cases: A tax preparer was given a person's papers in order to prepare the tax return, but the preparer's office was broken into and the steel filing cabinet in which the taxpayer's worksheets were stored was stolen. A taxpayer gave original documents to his attorney, who left them in his car overnight on a New York City street, with predictable results. A taxpayer gave his receipts, paid bills, and the like during the course of a tax audit to a Revenue Agent, who lost them.

8. *When you file your tax return, affix the label which I.R.S. has sent to you.* If you filed a federal income tax return last year, the Internal Revenue Service will send you a packet of blank tax forms to be used for filing this year's returns. This contains a pre-addressed sticker containing your name and address. It also has your Social Security number, which

many persons write on their returns from memory, sometimes incorrectly. The label also contains various coded material which helps the Service, such as type of return and the I.R.S. district where the taxpayer lives. This coding enables the Service to sort incoming tax returns electronically and to process them more rapidly. Processing a return with attached label costs 3¢, says the Service, while the cost if you fail to affix the label is 12¢.

If you are entitled to a refund, you'll get it sooner if this procedure is followed.

Each check you send to the Internal Revenue Service should have noted upon it your Social Security account number and reference to the taxable period involved and the type of tax.

Notify both the United States Postal Service and the Internal Revenue Service of a change of address, so that communications from the I.R.S. will reach you in time for prompt action by you. If you are to be away for any length of time, have someone check your incoming mail regularly to see whether there are any communications from the Service which should be sent to you, or made known to you, without delay. If enough is involved, give someone whom you trust a power of attorney to act for you during a lengthy absence, whether you are on an extended trip or in a hospital. You may choose to request that the I.R.S. send to your attorney copies of any communications which are sent to you.

9. *Remember that it's in your interest to get along with the Internal Revenue Service.* Familiar in military circles is the tale of the young second lieutenant who had just been assigned to his first post of duty. He correctly presented himself to the colonel, and a short conversation ensued. At its conclusion, the second lieutenant declared, ''I'm sure we are going to get along just fine, sir.'' ''Any getting along that's to be done,'' retorted the colonel, ''is your business.''

Even though it is to be anticipated that the Revenue Agent assigned to your case will be polite and considerate, *you* are the one who must do the getting along. The Revenue Agent does not have to do anything except ask questions. The taxpayer has to supply answers, explanations, reconciliations, back-up documentation. It is the taxpayer who must show that he is correct, that his records are adequate, current, and worthy of belief. They must clearly reflect his income. Missing records or documents are presumed not to have been produced upon request because it was against the taxpayer's interest to produce them.

A Revenue Agent is not a lone operator who can be overawed by a taxpayer's business or social status, personality, lawyers, and imposing experts. Remember that the Internal Revenue Service has the largest assemblage of data processing equipment in the world, the second largest law department in the nation. It has subpoena, summons, and other inquisitorial powers. But perhaps most important of all, in virtually every instance you are likely to encounter, the tax law presumes that the Service is correct. An I.R.S. "finding" is presumed to be correct, unless you can prove otherwise.

10. *Take dates seriously.* Make certain that tax return forms, schedules, refund claims, and appeals are filed on time and that you can prove it. Stockpile tax forms and schedules so that they are on hand when needed.

Anticipate filing times by rounding up in advance all necessary data as to payments you received in the form of salaries, fees, interest, dividends, sales of stock, and the like. See that you get receipts from charitable organizations and from physicians who require payment in cash. Make certain that dependents supply you with data as to their income and their total support costs, so that you can prove you contributed more than half of this support. This may require time in the case of reluctant relatives who resent intrusions into their private lives.

One little day means the difference between filing a tax return or other document on time and violating the law. In countless situations, the courts have held that one day means the difference between compliance and noncompliance. Even the courts cannot extend a filing or other compliance date spelled out in the tax law.

11. *Get it on the record contemporaneously.* The police should be advised of thefts and embezzlements at once to establish that the event took place under the circumstances alleged. Make note of officers' shield numbers as evidence of this. The insurance company should be sent a proof of claim loss promptly in the case of fires, floods, etc.

If a person uses a diary or other journal to substantiate his deductions, the entries are acceptable only if made at the very time of the expenditure. Courts have held that notations made in a business diary in the office on Monday of church contributions on Sunday lacked the required condition of contemporary recording. Where a businessperson has *bona fide* entertainment expenses, any recording of these must be of a strictly contemporary nature.

12. *Keep your cool in dealing with the Internal Revenue Service.* If a taxpayer permits himself to be worn down by the system, he is not likely to be able to defend himself properly. He may utter remarks which undermine his credibility, which disclose more than he had intended, which

call for reprisals in kind in the form of demands which otherwise might not have been made. A taxpayer's feeling of resentment at having a deduction questioned or at being pressed to supply seemingly endless information may take the form of anger and defiance which could be equated with interference with the administration of internal revenue laws.

A taxpayer's willingness to comply with the requirements is destroyed by words such as these which were reported in one decision: "Next year I'll do it, but next year never comes."

In a fraud matter, the Internal Revenue Service has to prove that a taxpayer had understated income by willfully evading taxes known to be due. In one case, a taxpayer proved this himself. When a Revenue Agent asked him if he knew what the tax law said about unfiled returns, he burst out: "Well, I will tell you. It is a Goddamn fraud, and what I did, I did deliberately."

Angry taxpayers have made threats against Revenue Agents and their families, which is a crime, even though a lesser one than if the threat is actually carried out. When Internal Revenue Service agents seize a taxpayer's property for nonpayment of taxes, it is a criminal act to seize it back even if the original seizure was not justified. There are other ways of seeking tax justice than direct action.

What to Avoid

In order to be a good taxpayer, knowing what not to do is no less important than knowing what to do. Here are eleven essential rules as to what to avoid:

1. *Don't make it impossible for your tax preparer to file a proper return.* When you turn over your papers to an accountant or other party at year-end, don't overlook (deliberately or otherwise) to give him everything which he must have to prepare an accurate income tax return for you. It is the taxpayer's responsibility to file accurate returns. He "may not foist that responsibility onto an agent," declared a 1980 decision.

2. *Don't use a fly-by-night tax preparer.* Remember always that it is *your* name which is signed on the tax return, whether or not a preparer also affixes his signature, which he is required to do if he receives a fee. (One professional tax preparer signed his name to a client's return in disappearing ink, but the Internal Revenue Service was able to identify him—as it very much wanted to do in this case—through the use of infrared light.) Beware of the preparer who guarantees in advance, before he sees your figures, that he will save you $X or Y%, or who manufac-

tures dependents for you to claim. The law requires professional preparers to keep addressed lists of clients; and if a preparer is found, by I.R.S. agents seeking for just such things, to be committing "irregularities" every one of his clients' returns is going to be examined very, very carefully. In addition, the work of a preparer without adequate credentials of experience and training is not likely to satisy the Service, even if no deliberate fraud was intended.

3. *Don't try to impress the Revenue Agent by telling him of your pipelines to higher authority, such as the Commissioner of Internal Revenue himself.* In his official capacity, the Revenue Agent probably has better pipelines than you do. In addition to being of dubious utility, comments to the Agent about your powerful connections are likely to be interpreted as threats, intimidation, or attempts to interfere with the administration of the tax law.

4. *Don't volunteer anything.* Tell the Revenue Agent what he asks you, checking, if you feel the need, with a lawyer knowledgeable in this area if there is a question about what you don't have to reveal. But if you say more than is asked for, you may say too much and lead the examiner to something which otherwise he never would have asked.

It is foolhardy to make statements involving matters which have not come under scrutiny. If a person mentions that because of a fire, his records were destroyed, this may lead to inquiries about perfectly proper deductions which the Agent will have to disallow because you do not have the necessary voucher, receipt, or cancelled check. Don't give the examiner any ideas as to where he is apt to find pay dirt, such as boasting about the fact that you haven't missed a Super Bowl game or heavyweight championship bout in many years. He may want to know how you reported these expenditures in your records.

5. *Don't be cute.* A very common example of this is the person who keeps secrets from his own accountant. If one conceals receipts of income or the existence of bank accounts from the person who prepares his financial statements or federal income tax returns, or even from his own partners or fellow executives, the Internal Revenue Service is likely to label the transaction as fraud: willful attempt to evade taxes known to be due.

The individual who advises his friends to treat income items the same way he does "so that those tax people never will find them" is helping other persons to evade taxes.

One taxpayer claimed a deduction which he called "I.R.S. Harassment" on his income tax return. How he determined the amount mathematically was not explained. Perhaps he helped himself psychologically by letting off steam. But he was penalized for claiming a deduction without attempting to find out whether he was entitled to take it.

A married woman filed her income tax return on an individual basis. She claimed an exemption for her husband, who was listed as a dependent child. Realistically, she may have been correct. But she was fined for disregard of the tax regulations.

6. *Don't say, "No one ever questioned it when I had the same thing last year."* Consistency in tax matters is not a virtue if you were wrong the first time. If you were wrong in your treatment of certain items in previous years, you have not changed that fact by repetition of the error. In addition to inviting the Internal Revenue Service to disallow the items of the same nature in all preceding years not yet closed by the statute of limitations, you may be suggesting to supervisors in your local district office that the persons who had examined your earlier returns had been incompetent—or worse. You may in effect be asking for a re-examination of all earlier tax returns which still are "open" for a second look.

7. *Don't deliberately leave something for a Revenue Agent to find.* Frequently one is given the advice that it is a good idea to have some modest item incorrectly handled on the tax return in an obvious place, so that an examiner is certain to find it. The theory is that if the Revenue Agent quickly finds something to disallow, he has justified the time spent on the examination and can report to his superiors proudly that he came home with a tax deficiency. This ploy probably will misfire. If a Revenue Agent discovers something which has been handled improperly with so little effort, probably he will conclude that if he really digs into the return, there will be much more for him to find. Now he'll have reason to do a thorough job.

8. *Don't think that anything is too small.* Just because something on the tax return is of very modest size, don't conclude that the Revenue Agent will not ask for substantiation. If a deduction is worth claiming in the first place, it is worth documenting so that there will not be a disallowance, with a possible penalty to be added, plus interest.

In one case, the court observed that a taxpayer's argument "contains a wistful aside that there is involved a large tax and only a small discrepancy. We are not moved, legally or emotionally, by this fact." In another case, an individual lost the dependency exemption he had claimed for his mother because the gross income that may be earned by someone claimed as a dependent ($1,000 for years after 1979) had been exceeded by $8.

9. *Don't talk about your affairs with anyone other than your advisor.* A person is inviting unnecessary tax trouble if he boasts to members of

the car pool, the in-laws, or anyone else of the successful "killings" he had in business or in the market. Or he may mention with a sly grin that he always charges ringside tickets when he takes his son to the fights to the good old expense account. Perhaps this is sheer fiction to impress folks. Or the entertaining really may be business-related and properly documented. But can this be *proven* when suspicious Internal Revenue Service personnel receive "squeal letters" or tips from would-be informants? Even if you think that everything is in proper order, it is pointless to invite Big Trouble. An examination can require considerable time and inconvenience, to say nothing of cost. One thing can lead to another. Keep your mouth as well as your desk drawer locked. Somebody may not like you, or he may be jealous of your success.

10. *Don't underestimate a Revenue Agent.* Examples of the ingenuity and persistence of tax examiners, as revealed in actual cases, were given in Chapter 9. But this warning is well worth repeating in any list of Don't's.

11. *Don't throw anything away.* This may be the most difficult of all recommendations to follow. The fact remains, however, that acceptance of an item on your federal income tax return may well depend upon whether somebody kept a little old piece of paper many years ago. For example, a descendant who is as yet unborn may have been given a copy of this book by you. In order to determine the amount of his gain when eventually he sells the volume to a rare book dealer, he will have to know how much you paid for it. Hopefully, no one will have thrown away the invoice.

Index

171

Index

Index